Geography

FOCUS
on Economics

George G. Watson, Jr.

Vernon Domingo

Margaret Landman

Glenn Miller

Carlyjane D. Watson

Martha C. Hopkins

OVER **45** YEARS
National Council
on Economic Education
SINCE 1949

Economics America
National Council on
Economic Education

A partnership of education,
business, and labor

AUTHORS

George G. Watson, Jr.
Executive Director
Economic Education Council of Massachusetts

Vernon Domingo
Professor of Geography
Bridgewater State College

Margaret Landman
Professor of Economics
Bridgewater State College

Glenn Miller
Professor of Geography
Bridgewater State College

Carlyjane D. Watson
Grade 8 Teacher
Bourne, Massachusetts Public Schools

Martha C. Hopkins, *Contributing Editor*
Field Coordinator
Center for Economic Education
University of Kansas

ISBN 1-56183-491-2

5 4 3 2 1

CONTENTS

FOREWORD

Geography: Focus on Economics, a core volume in a new generation of National Council publications, is dedicated to increasing the economic literacy of *all* students. The *Focus* publications, the new centerpiece of **Economics**America, build on almost five decades of success in delivering economic education to America's students.

The *Focus* series is both new and innovative, using economics primarily to enhance learning in subjects such as history, geography, civics, and personal finance. Activities are interactive, reflecting the belief that students learn best through active, highly personalized experiences with economics. Applications of economic understanding to real world situations and contexts dominate the lessons. In addition, the lessons explicitly teach the voluntary national standards in economics, outlined in the National Council's *A Framework for Teaching the Basic Economic Concepts.*

People look at the world from varying personal perspectives shaped by complex combinations of personal experience, occupational roles, self-interest, and community interest. The disciplines of economics and geography contain other perspec-tives that provide different frames of reference for asking and answering questions, identifying and solving problems, and evaluating the consequences of alternative actions. In *Geography: Focus on Economics* students use two specific geographic perspectives—spacial and ecological—to help them understand spacial patterns and processes and the interaction of living and nonliving elements in complex webs of relationships within nature and between nature and society.

Michael Watts, Professor of Economics, Purdue University, and Senior Fellow, National Council on Economic Education, reviewed the manuscript and offered many valuable suggestions. The authors and the publisher are responsible for the final publication.

The National Council thanks the authors, George Watson, Vernon Domingo, Margaret Landman, Glenn Miller, and Carlyjane Watson for their engaging presentation of the connections between economics and geography. We also thank Martha Hopkins for her work as contributing editor. We recognize, as well, the financial support of the National Science Foundation.

Joan Sullivan Baranski
Publisher

ACKNOWLEDGMENTS

The National Council on Economic Education recognizes the contributions of many people involved in this project. The council staff and authors offer special thanks to the following people who helped plan and evaluate the materials.

Richard Aieta, member of the oversight committee for the National Geography Standards, social studies department head, Hamilton-Wenham High School, South Hamilton, Massachusetts, who provided the inspiration for the Geo-Poem Activity.

Robert C. Watson, geologist with GZA GeoEnvironmental, Inc., Portland, Maine, who provided technical assistance in the preparation of the Lancaster Landfill Activity.

TEACHER ADVISORY COMMITTEE

Helena Anzivino, grade 6, Rogers Middle School, Rockland, Massachusetts
Amy-Jo Aronson, grade 6, Rogers Middle School, Rockland, Massachusetts
Patti Barry, grade 6, Forestdale School, Forestdale, Massachusetts
Mary J. Bettencourt, social studies, Memorial Junior High, Middleboro, Massachusetts
Michelle Dunn, grade 6, Mattacheese Middle School, W. Yarmouth, Massachusetts
Mary Beth Dunphe, grade 7 world geography, Oakridge School, East Sandwich, Massachusetts
John Enos, principal, Sacred Heart Junior High, Kingston, Massachusetts
Stephen Gardiner, Economics Department, Bridgewater State College
Randy Hoover, grade 7 world geography, Forestdale School, Forestdale, Massachusetts
Charles Horbert, Norton Middle School, Norton, Massachusetts
Eileen Joyce, Memorial Junior High School, Middleboro, Massachusetts
Barbara Kimball, grade 7, Mattacheese Middle School, W. Yarmouth, Massachusetts
Kathy Lennox, grade 5, Forestdale School, Forestdale, Massachusetts

Joe Masi, Sacred Heart Junior High, Kingston, Massachusetts
Dennis McGee, grade 7 geography, Randolph High School, Randolph, Massachusetts
Tom Ruest, Norton Middle School, Norton, Massachusetts
Norm Shacochis, Scituate High School, Scituate, Massachusetts
Angelo Veneziano, Federal Reserve Bank of Boston, Boston, Massachusetts

REVIEWER

Michael Watts, Purdue University, made numerous suggestions that significantly improved the economic content and analysis in the lessons. Other reviewers included Robert Catus, George Dawson, Lowell Harriss, Mary Suiter, and Donna Wright.

CONTRIBUTING EDITOR

Martha Hopkins, Field Coordinator, Center for Economic Education, University of Kansas, did an outstanding job of editing these materials and contributed many ideas that improved the instructional quality of the lessons.

INTRODUCTION

OVERVIEW

Geography and economics are included as core subjects in Goals 2000: Educate America Act. The Geography Education Standards Project has prepared *Geography for Life: National Geography Standards 1994*, and the project to create national economics standards is about to begin. The two disciplines have much in common. Each is a social science that relies upon basic critical-thinking skills. While each has its own concepts, skills, tools, and technologies, there is considerable overlap. For example, resources, their distribution, and use are important to both.

The National Council on Economic Education's *A Framework for Teaching Basic Economic Concepts with Scope and Sequence Guidelines, K–12*, advocates economic education programs that will help students to become productive members of the work force, responsible citizens, knowledgeable consumers, prudent savers and investors, effective participants in a global economy, and competent decision makers throughout their lives.

These same performance outcomes are echoed throughout *Geography for Life: National Geography Standards 1994*. According to that publication, geographic literacy is essential if students are to leave school prepared for productive employment, responsible citizenship, effective participation in a global economy, and competent decision making.

The 12 lessons in this publication are only a small sample of the many ways that geography and economics can be integrated. While each lesson stands on its own, all lessons are organized around four themes.

ECONOMIC AND GEOGRAPHIC PERSPECTIVES

People look at the world from varying personal perspectives shaped by complex combinations of personal experience, occupational roles, self-interest, and community interest. They enhance their knowledge and skills by learning to view the world from additional perspectives. The disciplines of economics and geography contain perspectives that provide frames of reference for asking and answering questions, identifying and solving problems, and evaluating the consequences of alternative actions.

Two specific geographic perspectives are the spatial perspective and the ecological perspective. An understanding of spatial patterns and processes on Earth and the interaction of living and non-living elements in complex webs of relationships within nature and between nature and societies is central to geography. Information about people, places, and environments can be acquired, organized, and analyzed using maps and other geographic tools to provide a spatial perspective. Where something exists or occurs and why it is there are important dimensions of the physical world and the human activities that take place on its surface. A spatial perspective is helpful to people deciding where to buy or rent a home, how to get to work, and where to shop. When businesses choose locations for retail stores or manufacturing plants, or communities pick sites for schools, landfills, and prisons, their decisions usually involve spatial perspectives.

An ecological perspective helps people understand how human actions affect the physical environment and how the physical world and physical processes affect human activities. For example, when a power plant generates electricity by burning coal and thus polluting the air, which results in acid rain that falls into a lake many miles away, an ecosystem may be damaged, and fish in the lake may die. People living near the lake may be deprived of a source of food and fresh water. An ecological perspective is useful also in identifying the possible consequences of farming or building houses on a floodplain, the role of auto emissions in creating air pollution and atmospheric warming, the effect of the use of chemicals upon the depletion of the ozone layer, and the impact of all these activities on people's health and well-being.

People can also view the world from an economic perspective. Economics focuses on how people use scarce resources to produce and exchange goods and services to satisfy human wants. Scarcity requires people to make choices about how best to utilize available resources. All societies must make the basic economic decisions of what goods and services to produce, how to produce these goods and services, and how to divide these goods and services among their members. Since many of the human actitivies that modify the physical environment are the result of societies using scarce resources to produce goods and services, an economic perspective can be very valuable to students of geography.

The first two lessons introduce students to economic and geographic perspectives.

GEOGRAPHY AND INTERNATIONAL TRADE

The spatial dimensions of economic activity and global interdependence are visible everywhere. The international economic concepts of comparative advantage, exchange rates, and trade restrictions are more important today than in the past.

The United States is the world's largest trading nation, providing 12 to 15% of the goods and services that other nations purchase. International trade is an increasingly important part of the U.S. economy. U.S. imports and exports have risen from a total of 9.4% of real GDP in 1960 to 24.8% in 1993 and may reach 40% within the present decade.

The quantity and quality of productive resources available in different nations vary widely. When nations specialize in producing those goods and services for which they have comparative advantages, international trade increases, resulting in a more efficient allocation of world resources and an increase in total world output.

Despite the benefits of international trade, many nations restrict the free flow of goods and services through a variety of devices known as trade barriers. Tariffs, quotas, embargoes, licensing requirements, health and safety standards, and subsidies are the most frequently used instruments of trade restriction.

In lessons 3 through 6 students explore geography and international trade.

ANALYSIS OF GEOGRAPHIC AND ECONOMIC INFORMATION

Geographic and economic skills help people make reasoned decisions. It is important to be able to ask geographic and economic questions, acquire geographic and economic information, organize geographic and economic information, analyze geographic and economic information, and answer geographic and economic questions.

Maps and graphs are essential tools for developing these skills, because they assist in the visualization of space. The "where" of the map is added to the "what" of the data. Choropleth maps, cartograms, and population pyramids are frequently used by geographers.

Choropleth maps apply a spatial perspective to economic and social data. Choropleth maps are maps that show differences between areas by using colors or shading to represent distinct categories of variables such as Gross Domestic Product (GDP), life expectancy, and population density.

Cartograms are maps that use population, Gross Domestic Product (GDP), or some other property to determine the size of an area, unlike conventional maps, which usually depict the area based on square miles. They can be a very effective way to present geographic and economic data.

Population pyramids are bar graphs showing the distribution by gender and age of an area's (town, state, nation, or region, for example) population. Population pyramids are relatively easy to construct and are used frequently to predict business opportunities and to plan for an appropriate mix of those goods and services usually provided by government agencies.

Lessons 7 through 10 teach students to analyze geographic and economic information using these maps and graphs.

APPLICATION OF ECONOMIC AND GEOGRAPHIC PERSPECTIVES

Places change over time as both physical and

human processes interact to modify the earth's surface. Knowing how and why places change is important for understanding how places came to be the way they are.

Both economics and geography are concerned with the similarities and differences among places. Both are concerned about how best to use available resources. Geographers are especially concerned about what economists call externalities. Externalities exist when some of the costs or benefits associated with the production or consumption of a product "spill over" to third parties other than the direct producers and consumers of the product. Positive externalities (external benefits) result in the underproduction or underconsumption of a product, since not all benefits are reflected in consumers' demand for the product. Negative externalities (external costs) result in the overproduction or overconsumption of a product, since not all costs are reflected in producers' supply of the product. It is in this area that the geographer's ecological perspective can inform the economist's judgments about how to use available resources.

Lessons 11 and 12 ask students to apply economic and geographic perspectives.

ABILITY GUIDELINES AND FLEXIBILITY OF TEXT

Geography: Focus on Economics is suitable for a wide variety of curriculum needs and teaching strategies. The program allows for great flexibility in teaching and learning—offering ample support for students of different ability levels. As there is no single approach or method adequate in all situations, the authors suggest many approaches for teachers to choose from to best suit the needs of their individual courses and to match the abilities, interests, and backgrounds of students. In general, the lessons are for all students.

KEY TO ABILITY LEVELS

The following coding system identifies activities suitable for students of various ability levels:
  ★ all students—basic course material
  ■ average and above average students
  ○ average and below average students

LESSON ONE
WHERE IN THE WORLD?

INTRODUCTION

Global economic interdependence is a reality. People and businesses in the United States buy goods, services, and productive resources produced in other countries. People throughout the world sell goods, services, and productive resources to earn income, which can be used to purchase products produced in other countries. A country's **exports** are the goods and services it produces and sells to buyers in another country.

Goods are objects that can satisfy people's wants. Shoes and tennis racquets are goods. **Services** are activities that can satisfy people's wants. Ocean cruises and concerts are examples of services.

Productive resources are all natural resources, human resources, and capital resources used in the production of goods and services. **Natural resources** are "gifts of nature" that are present without human intervention. Land, water, and crude oil deposits are natural resources. **Human resources** (also called labor) are the efforts of people toward producing goods and services. **Capital resources** are goods made by people and used to produce other goods and services. Tractors, factories, and carpenter tools are capital resources.

Renewable resources are resources that can be regenerated if used carefully. Grains, timber, and fish are renewable resources. **Nonrenewable resources** are finite and cannot be replaced once they are used up. Copper, tin, and natural gas are nonrenewable resources.

In international as in domestic markets, prices provide information to buyers and sellers, encouraging the efficient production and allocation of goods, services, and productive resources. Changes in the relative scarcity of goods, services, and productive resources will lead to price

changes, and buyers and sellers will respond to those changes.

To be geographically informed, people should understand the patterns and networks of economic interdependence. To know where something exists or occurs is to use the geographic **spatial perspective**. Location and place are concepts that are used to provide a spatial perspective. **Location** is the position something occupies on the earth's surface. A **place** is a location having distinctive characteristics that give it meaning and distinguish it from other locations. The place where a country's government is located is called the **national capital**.

How life forms interact with the physical environment is the geographic **ecological perspective**. For example, people who express general concern about the depletion of nonrenewable resources are using an ecological perspective. These people will improve their understanding of the situation by using an **economic perspective** and knowing how competitive markets will allocate these resources as available supplies become more scarce.

Atlases are useful tools for acquiring geographic information, and maps are useful for presenting data systematically. This lesson uses both to identify selected countries that export specific resources and products.

CONCEPTS

Exports
Goods
Services
Productive Resources
Natural Resources
Human Resources
Capital Resources
Renewable Resources
Nonrenewable Resources
Spatial Perspective
Location
Place
National Capital
Ecological Perspective
Economic Perspective
Consumer Goods

OBJECTIVES

◆ Recognize that the productive resources available in different nations vary widely.

◆ Identify selected countries that export specific goods, services, and productive resources.

◆ Use an atlas to match national capitals with their countries.

◆ Locate countries and their capitals on a world map.

◆ Classify exports as consumer goods or productive resources

◆ Classify resources as renewable or nonrenewable.

◆ Hypothesize reasons for trading nonrenewable resources.

◆ Hypothesize choices available to buyers and sellers when nonrenewable resources are being exhausted.

LESSON DESCRIPTION

Students participate in a bingo-type game to learn the national capitals of countries exporting specific resources and products, use prior knowledge and atlases to identify the countries involved, and locate both the countries and their capitals on a world map. They classify the goods and resources being traded and discuss the choices that sellers and buyers make.

TIME REQUIRED

Two class periods. (The map may be completed as homework.)

MATERIALS

★ One copy for each student of Activity 1, *Where in the World?*
★ One copy of Activity 2, *Export Cards*
★ One copy for each student of Activity 3, *Bingo Card*
A blank sheet of paper for each student
An outline world map for each student (Activity 4)
As many student atlases as available

PROCEDURE

1. Tell the class that this lesson focuses on products that are traded among nations. They will use geographic and economic perspectives to locate these nations, to classify these products, and to discuss the choices that buyers and sellers are making and might make in the future.

2. Distribute cards cut from Activity 2, *Export Cards*, giving one card to each student. Explain that a country's exports are the goods and services that it produces and sells to buyers in other countries. Distribute Activity 1, *Where in the World?*, Activity 3, *Bingo Card*, an outline world map, and a blank sheet of paper to each student. Ask the class to read Activity 1, *Where in the World?*

3. When everyone has finished reading, explain the following rules for playing Export Bingo:

• Use the blank sheet of paper to make a sign that advertises the product on your export card.

• Circulate throughout the room to trade information with other students. Record the capitals associated with the exported products in the spaces provided on your bingo card. When you have collected all the capitals, use your knowledge and the atlases available in the classroom to fill in the names of the countries in the spaces on your bingo card.

• When your bingo card is complete, transfer the information to the world map. Use the atlases to find the locations of the capitals and mark them with dots on the map. Record the rest of the information as best you can, using arrows pointing to the country if the space on the map is too small for the information to fit.

(If you think it will be difficult for some of your students to complete this activity, you may wish to divide the class into small groups once they have entered all of the national capitals on their bingo cards. Using the atlases and completing the maps will then become a cooperative learning activity. This procedure will also reduce the number of atlases and outline world maps required by the activity.)

Answers for Bingo Card
(Activity 3)

EXPORT	CAPITAL	COUNTRY
Gold	Pretoria	South Africa
Oil	Riyadh	Saudi Arabia
Rubber	Kuala Lumpur	Malaysia
Copper	Santiago	Chile
Bauxite	Paramaribo	Suriname
Wood	Ottawa	Canada
Phosphates	Rabat	Morocco
Aluminum	Kingston	Jamaica
Uranium	Niamey	Niger
Jute	Dhaka	Bangladesh
Autos	Tokyo	Japan
Fruit	Madrid	Spain
Sugar	Manila	Philippines
Cocoa	Accra	Ghana
Coffee	Bogota	Colombia
Cotton	Mexico City	Mexico
Clothing	Seoul	South Korea
Tea	Colombo	Sri Lanka
Tin	La Paz	Bolivia
Rice	Bangkok	Thailand
Machinery	Stockholm	Sweden
Fish	Reykjavik	Iceland
Copra	Apia	Western Samoa
Polished Diamonds	Jerusalem	Israel
Meat	Wellington	New Zealand
Natural Gas	Algiers	Algeria
Bananas	Tegucigalpa	Honduras
Precision Instruments	Bern	Switzerland
Iron Ore	Nouakchott	Mauritania
Textiles	Paris	France

4. When the students have completed their maps, ask them how they acquired the information that linked the products to national capitals. (They traded the information they had on their export cards for it.) Point out that this is the nature of all voluntary trade. Both parties to the trade believe they are gaining by trading or they will not make the trade.

5. Conduct a class discussion based on Activity 1, *Where in the World?* and the definitions provided here. State the definition and write it on the board or a transparency in each case.

- *Consumer goods and services* are products and activities purchased by households for final consumption.

- *Productive resources* are all natural resources, human resources, and human-made resources (capital) used in the production of goods and services.

Ask the students which of the exports on their Bingo Cards could be used both ways. (It is the use to which the good is put that determines whether a good is a consumer good; not the characteristics of the good itself. A computer purchased for the home is a consumer good; the same computer purchased for a business is a productive resource or a producer good. Many of the products may be listed in more than one category. Do not let the discussion become argumentative. If a student's answer is challenged, ask for a defense based on the definitions provided in the activity and move on.)

6. State the following definitions and write them on the board or a transparency.

- *Renewable resources* are resources that can be regenerated if used carefully.

- *Nonrenewable resources* are finite and cannot be replaced once they are used up.

Ask the class:

Which of the exports on the Bingo Card use productive resources that are renewable? (Rubber, wood, jute, fruit, sugar, cocoa, coffee, cotton, tea, rice, fish, copra, meat, and bananas. Clothing and textiles are likely to be made from renewable resources.)

Which of the exports on the Bingo Card use productive resources that are nonrenewable? (Gold, oil, copper, bauxite, phosphates, aluminum, uranium, tin, diamonds, natural gas, and iron ore. Autos, machinery, and precision instruments are likely to contain some nonrenewable resources.)

CLOSURE

Put the list of nonrenewable resources on the board or on a transparency. Ask students to suggest other nonrenewable resources to add to the list.

Remind the class that exports are traded voluntarily. A seller in one country finds a buyer in another country, and a sale is made. Then ask the following questions:

- Why would anyone want to sell a nonrenewable resource? (These resources are not distributed uniformly. In places where they are plentiful and where there is relatively low demand for them, sellers choose to export them in order to obtain income to buy other products. Voluntary trade takes place only when a buyer and a seller both expect to be better off for having made the trade. Sometimes people make bad bargains and would like to undo a trade they have made, and sometimes people are uncertain about the benefits they will gain. They have a great deal of confidence that they will gain from trades that they make frequently and have made many times before. The reasons for selling nonrenewable resources are the same as those for selling renewable resources.)

- What choices might buyers and sellers make when available supplies of a nonrenewable resource are becoming more scarce? (Sellers may choose to take advantage of rising prices and sell their resources, or hold on to their resources in anticipation of still higher prices in the future. They can "mine" less productive areas or process ores with lower yields at higher costs, because the higher prices make it profitable to do so. They can increase spending in search of new sources of the resources. Buyers may choose to do without the resource, change production techniques to reduce waste, use recycled resources, find substitutes for the resource, or pay the higher prices. Both sellers and buyers will respond to incentives such as higher prices, profits, and government regulations.)

EVALUATION

- Divide the students into cooperative groups. Ask each group to make a list of goods and services that they have purchased that were produced in other countries. Ask each group member to choose one of the items from the list and to write a paragraph that includes where the good or service was produced, what

productive resources were used to produce it, whether a similar good or service produced in the United States was available, and why this good or service was purchased. (If writing individual paragraphs is too difficult for your students, let each *group* write a paragraph.)

EXTENSION ACTIVITIES

1. Students can select countries that they have studied and use their geography textbooks, appropriate atlases, encyclopedias, and other sources to identify the countries' major trading partners. They can locate these trading partners on a map and write brief reports suggesting possible reasons for the pattern of trade they have discovered through their research.

2. Students can use newspaper and periodical articles to identify possible causes of recent world trade interruptions such as war, crop failure due to weather and other factors, natural disasters, and strikes and write brief reports on the impacts of such interruptions in various parts of the world.

3. Students can research any of the resources from the Bingo Card and report on the location of the resource, the uses for the resource, and the characteristics of the world market for the resource. (Where is it found? What is it used for? Who sells it? Who buys it? How much is bought and sold? At what prices?)

ACTIVITY 1
WHERE IN THE WORLD?

A perspective is a way of looking at things. Everyone looks at the world from a personal perspective. Your personal perspective is shaped by a combination of personal experiences, self-interest, and interests shared with others. Your roles as a family member, as a student in your school, and as a resident in your community, state, and nation affect the way you view the world. You share cultural perspectives with other members of your age, gender, religious, racial, and ethnic groups. Your perspectives can either help or hinder you in understanding and dealing with the many decisions you have to make every day. If you view the world using only one or a few of your perspectives, you limit yourself. Learning to understand the world from many perspectives will increase your knowledge and skills.

The study of geography and economics provides perspectives that can help you to ask and answer questions, identify and solve problems, and think about the possible consequences of the choices available to you. There are two important geographic perspectives. One is the *spatial perspective* which looks at location, where something is, and why it is there. Places can be located on the earth's surface using a grid system or their positions may be described relative to the positions of other places. Each place has special characteristics that give it meaning and distinguish it from other places. One such place is a national capital, which is the city where the government of a country is officially located. The other geographic perspective is called the *ecological perspective*. This views the earth as a set of living and nonliving elements that interact on many levels.

There is also an *economic perspective*. Economics focuses on how people use scarce resources to produce and exchange goods and services to satisfy their wants. *Goods* are objects such as bicycles and pizzas, and *services* are activities such as lawn mowing and hair styling. Individuals and societies face choices about what goods and services to produce, how to use available resources to produce these goods and services, and how to share the goods and services that are produced. You live in a world where local, regional, and national economies are a part of a global economy. You buy some products that were produced thousands of miles away from your home and other products that were made nearby using resources that came from distant lands. An economic perspective will help you to understand how people are connected through the trading of goods and services.

This lesson is about products that are traded among nations. You will use geographic and economic perspectives to locate these nations, to classify these products, and to discuss the choices that buyers and sellers are making now and choices they might make in the future.

ACTIVITY 2
EXPORT CARDS

GOLD Pretoria	OIL Riyadh	RUBBER Kuala Lumpur
COPPER Santiago	BAUXITE Paramaribo	WOOD Ottawa
PHOSPHATES Rabat	ALUMINUM Kingston	URANIUM Niamey
JUTE Dhaka	AUTOS Tokyo	FRUIT Madrid
SUGAR Manila	COCOA Accra	COFFEE Bogota
COTTON Mexico City	CLOTHING Seoul	TEA Colombo
TIN La Paz	RICE Bangkok	MACHINERY Stockholm
FISH Reykjavik	COPRA Apia	POLISHED DIAMONDS Jerusalem
MEAT Wellington	NATURAL GAS Algiers	BANANAS Tegucigalpa
PRECISION INSTRUMENTS Bern	IRON ORE Nouakchott	TEXTILES Paris

From *Geography: Focus on Economics,* © National Council on Economic Education, New York, NY

ACTIVITY 3
BINGO CARD

Name ______________________________

GOLD Capital ____ Country ____	**OIL** Capital ____ Country ____	**RUBBER** Capital ____ Country ____	**COPPER** Capital ____ Country ____	**BAUXITE** Capital ____ Country ____
WOOD Capital ____ Country ____	**PHOSPHATES** Capital ____ Country ____	**ALUMINUM** Capital ____ Country ____	**URANIUM** Capital ____ Country ____	**JUTE** Capital ____ Country ____
AUTOS Capital ____ Country ____	**FRUIT** Capital ____ Country ____	**SUGAR** Capital ____ Country ____	**COCOA** Capital ____ Country ____	**COFFEE** Capital ____ Country ____
COTTON Capital ____ Country ____	**CLOTHING** Capital ____ Country ____	**TEA** Capital ____ Country ____	**TIN** Capital ____ Country ____	**RICE** Capital ____ Country ____
MACHINERY Capital ____ Country ____	**FISH** Capital ____ Country ____	**COPRA** Capital ____ Country ____	**POLISHED DIAMONDS** Capital ____ Country ____	**MEAT** Capital ____ Country ____
NATURAL GAS Capital ____ Country ____	**BANANAS** Capital ____ Country ____	**PRECISION INSTRUMENTS** Capital ____ Country ____	**IRON ORE** Capital ____ Country ____	**TEXTILES** Capital ____ Country ____

ACTIVITY 4
WORLD MAP

ACTIVITY 4 (continued)
WORLD MAP

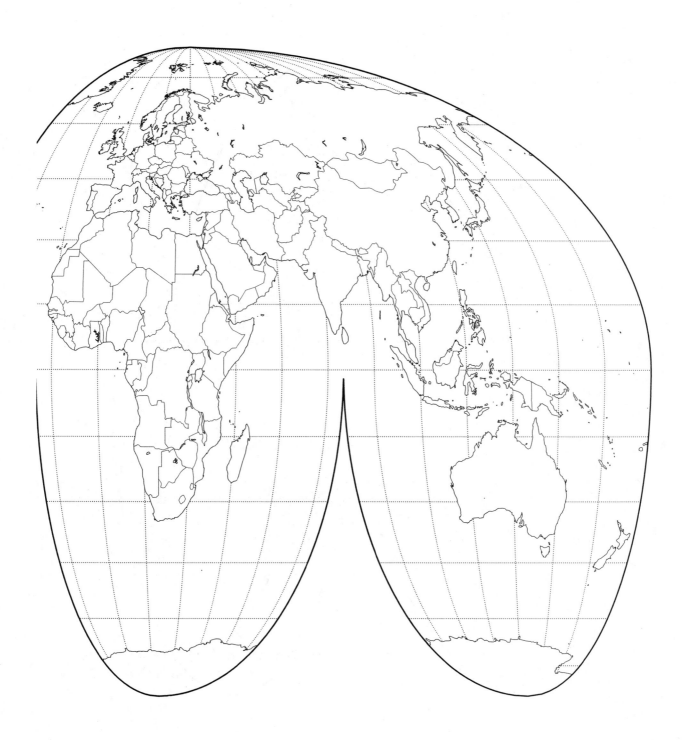

ACTIVITY 4 (continued)
WORLD MAP ANSWERS

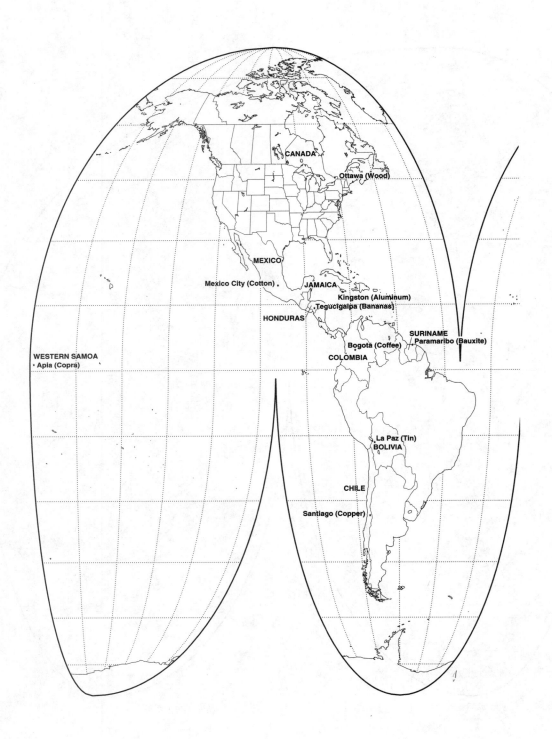

ACTIVITY 4 (continued)
WORLD MAP ANSWERS

ICELAND
Reykjavik (Fish)
SWEDEN
Stockholm (Machinery)
Paris (Textiles)
Bern (Precision Instruments)
FRANCE
SWITZ.
Madrid (Fruit)
SPAIN
Rabat (Phosphates)
Algers (Natural Gas)
MOROCCO
ISRAEL Jerusalem (Polished Diamonds)
ALGERIA
Riyadh (Oil)
MAURITANIA
Nouakchott (Iron Ore)
NIGER
SAUDI ARABIA
Niamey (Uranium)
Seoul (Clothing)
SOUTH KOREA
Tokyo (Autos)
JAPAN
Dhaka (Jute)
BANGLADESH
THAILAND
Bangkok (Rice)
Manila (Sugar)
PHILIPPINES
Accra (Cocoa)
SRI LANKA
Colombo(Tea)
MALAYSIA
GHANA
Kuala Lumpur (Rubber)
Pretoria (Gold)
SOUTH AFRICA
Wellington (Meat)
NEW ZEALAND

LESSON TWO
WHERE DO YOU SHOP?

INTRODUCTION

Shopping is a regular activity in most Americans' lives. Where people shop is influenced by personal knowledge, personal preferences, economic factors, and geographic factors.

Knowledge about a store may encourage or discourage people from shopping there. People are often reluctant to change where they shop because they are comfortable with the familiar. Acquiring knowledge about new stores takes time and must be considered to be a cost.

Preferences or tastes influence where people shop. People's perceptions of quality and good service will keep them coming to a store even after they move out of a neighborhood.

People's incomes and the relative prices of the goods and services they would like to buy affect their decisions about where to shop. People who place a high value upon their time based on what their time is worth in the workplace may consider the time spent acquiring a good or service and the time spent consuming it to be costs of the transaction. With some services, however, the length of time is part of the benefit, and customers are charged on that basis.

Time-distance, the amount of time necessary to travel between two places, is an important geographic factor. To be successful, stores must locate where there is a sufficiently large customer base with access to the stores. Specialized stores require high population density. The choice of location involves two major concepts: threshold and range. A **threshold** population is the minimum number of customers necessary for a store to stay in business. The concept **range** is the maximum distance and time people are willing to travel to purchase a good or service. In order for a store to succeed, its threshold population (customer base), must be within the range people are

willing to travel to purchase the particular good or service sold by that store.

CONCEPTS
Time-distance
Threshold
Range
Transaction Costs
Specialization

OBJECTIVES

◆ Examine the role of geography in personal purchases.

◆ Recognize the importance of threshold populations for business success.

◆ Identify differences in range for different products and services.

◆ Apply the concept of time-distance to modify the discussion of range.

◆ Understand the value of time as a transaction cost.

◆ Develop a method for assessing the value of their own time as a transaction cost.

◆ Recognize the importance of changing perceptions of distance on business success.

◆ Conduct interviews to acquire information

◆ Hypothesize changes in shopping patterns.

LESSON DESCRIPTION

Students use road maps to measure distances traveled to purchase specific goods and services, calculate average distances, and rank goods from shortest to longest distances traveled. They discuss the survey and its limitations, are introduced to the idea of time-value as a transaction cost, and offer ways of determining the value of their own time. They read about threshold, range, and specialization as factors that affect the location of businesses. They interview three persons of their grandparents' generation and compare shopping patterns during the older generation's childhood to today's patterns. Finally, they offer hypotheses about the changes catalog mail-order and phone sales, and home-shopping television programs will have on where people shop.

TIME REQUIRED

Two or three class periods.

MATERIALS

Calculators (optional)

A copy of a regional road map for each student. (The map should show the area within a twenty-mile radius of the school neighborhood. A smaller radius should be chosen if the school is situated in a densely populated area.)

Rulers (Enough for the class to share.)

★ One copy of Activity 1, *Where Do You Shop?*, for each student and one copy of Activity 2, *Where Did Your Grandparents Shop?*, for each student

Regional telephone directories (To look up addresses of businesses that students are not sure about.)

Visual 1, *Where We Shop*

PROCEDURE

1. Explain that this lesson focuses on where people shop for a variety of goods and services and why they shop where they do.

2. Distribute maps, rulers, and Activity 1, *Where Do You Shop?* Ask the students to read the activity and to follow the directions to complete the table. Explain that they should list the names of the stores or offices where they would purchase the goods and services listed in Activity 1, locate their homes and each of the businesses on their maps, use the rulers to measure the straight-line distances on the map from their homes to each of the locations, and use the map scale to calculate how far they would travel for each item.

3. After all students in the class have their distance measurements, use Visual 1, *Where We Shop* to record information, calculate class averages for each item, and rank the purchases from shortest trips to longest trips taken. (Use the transparency provided or copy it on the board. Ask one or two students to calculate the averages for each item.)

4. Ask the students the following questions:

- How would you make these trips? Would you walk, drive a car or be driven in a car, ride a bus or other form of public transportation, or hire a taxi? How might your mode of transportation affect your decisions about how far you would travel to purchase

Visual 1: Where We Shop (Sample)

Student	Family Groceries	Convenience Store Goods	Physician	Dentist	Clothing	Video Rental	Hair Styling	Recorded Music	Medical Supplies	Movie Tickets
MH	0.6	0.8	2.6	0.7	2.7	1.9	2.5	2.7	0.6	1.4
DJ	0.8	0.7	3.0	1.8	1.8	1.8	4.1	10.0	0.2	6.3
PB	19.5	0.5	6.0	19.5	19.5	3.0	10.0	9.5	0.5	7.0
LS	0.9	1.0	2.2	2.2	8.0	4.4	2.0	8.0	0.9	8.0
TC	0.3	3.4	5.0	4.2	0.6	5.4	0.4	8.9	5.2	8.9
MMck	1.7	0.2	7.2	3.0	6.2	2.4	1.5	5.1	1.5	4.5
SK	5.5	0.5	2.3	3.0	2.0	2.5	8.0	4.8	2.1	7.5
HW	0.9	0.4	1.4	1.8	1.7	3.4	1.0	3.7	0.2	3.6
MF	7.0	3.0	7.5	6.0	5.5	4.5	10.0	5.5	3.0	13.5
VA	3.2	1.0	0.9	1.0	5.2	0.9	4.2	5.3	1.1	3.1
CD	14.0	1.4	7.0	2.0	7.0	5.0	6.0	30.0	0.5	5.0
EM	0.8	1.0	4.2	1.8	2.0	0.4	1.4	2.2	1.2	3.0
ND	1.2	5.0	2.3	2.0	2.4	1.8	1.0	2.2	5.0	1.2
CS	2.0	0.2	4.0	20.0	15.0	3.4	5.0	6.0	1.0	5.0
AVERAGE	4.2	1.4	4.0	4.9	5.7	2.9	4.1	7.4	1.6	5.6
RANK	6	1	4	7	9	3	5	10	2	8

★ all students–basic course material
■ average and above average students
○ average and below average students

13

the items? (The availability of transportation when they want to make the trips, how close the mode of transportation brings them to the location, the size and weight of the items to be purchased, and the transportation costs would be some of the important factors.)

• Distances on the map were measured in straight lines. Would any of the locations you selected involve physical barriers such as rivers, swamps, hills, cemeteries, factories, or railroad tracks that you would have to go around? How would they affect the accuracy of the survey? (The distance to be traveled would be greater than the straight-line measure.)

• Is distance your only consideration when you go shopping, or aren't you concerned about the condition of the roads, traffic congestion, availability of parking, and availability of employees to wait on you? What is common to all of these concerns? (They affect the time it takes to purchase the item.)

5. Geographers use a concept called **time-distance**, the amount of time necessary to travel between two places. Write the term on the board and define it for the students. Ask the class how this concept could have been used in the class survey and what measurement problems it would have added to the activity. (It would have been a better measure of what consumers care about when deciding where to shop. It would have involved students deciding how they would travel to each location, making the trip using that mode of transportation at the various times they might shop, and making a judgment about the time it would take to complete the purchase. It wasn't practical to make these measurements, and students' estimates of time-distance would not have been very reliable.)

6. Economists would say that time-distance represents a transaction cost to consumers. Write *transaction costs* on the board and give the following explanation. **Transaction costs** include the cost of learning about a product's qualities, price, availability, safety, maintenance requirements, and other information about the product. Phone calls, library research, and visits to stores may be required before you buy a new stereo system. There are costs involved in negotiating the sale and signing contracts when you buy a home. Generally, highly organized markets such as stock exchanges have low transaction costs and less well organized markets such as private sales of used cars have relatively high transaction costs. Time has a value to each person. The cost to the consumer of any purchase should include, therefore, not only the price paid for the good or service but also the value of the time spent acquiring and consuming it. Retired persons with relatively low incomes and lots of time available will spend more time hunting for bargains than highly paid executives whose time is very valuable.

Ask the class how transaction costs might apply to Activity 1, *Where Do You Shop?* (The transaction costs of each good or service should be added to its price when one is deciding which of several items to purchase. A relatively high transaction cost might be unacceptable for an inexpensive product but acceptable for a more expensive item. People would be less likely to drive 30 miles or 90 minutes to buy a loaf of bread at a bargain price, but they would make the trip to save the same percentage on a new car.)

7. Ask the students how they would place a value on their time. (Some students have jobs and may quote an hourly wage rate. Some students may say that their job is studying, and their compensation is the grades they receive, so the transaction cost is the impact the time spent shopping has on their school achievement. Other students may use the value they place on their leisure time as a basis for computing the transaction cost of shopping.)

8. Ask the class whether anyone said he or she would buy two or more of the items at a shopping center or mall. Assuming that some students did, ask how that affects the accuracy of the survey. (If one trip is made and several items are bought, the distance should be divided by the number of transactions. This is already reflected in the survey that showed that people were willing to travel farther to purchase a weekly supply of groceries than to buy one or two items at a convenience store. Moreover, in some places the mall is

a sort of community center. Older persons walk around the mall for exercise before the stores open, and students meet with their friends at the mall. If one is already at the mall for other reasons, the transaction cost may be as low as the value of the time spent shopping for the product.)

CLOSURE

• Distribute Activity 2, *Where Did Your Grandparents Shop?* Explain the meaning of *threshold* and *range,* which are defined in the introduction to this lesson and explained in the first two paragraphs of the activity. Allow a few minutes for the students to read the narratives and answer questions they may have about the assignment. Assign a due date for the *Interview Summaries.* Students will need several days to complete the assignment.

• On the day the interview summaries are due, have several students read or summarize what they have written. (This is an activity that all students can do well. You may want to have them create posters to illustrate their interviews, using photographs of the people they interview, pictures from magazines, or their own artwork.) Discuss the changes that the students describe with their writing or posters.

• Ask the students if they or their families ever use catalogs to make purchases (either by mailing or phoning in orders). What are the threshold populations of these businesses and the ranges of buyers? How do next day mail and delivery services encourage these purchases? Will home-shopping programs or similar television services displace local businesses? (Catalogs reach millions of potential buyers of very specialized products. There are several companies who mail catalogs of over 100 pages at least twice a month in order to sell computer programs and accessories for owners of Macintosh computers. These companies accept credit card orders by phone and provide overnight delivery at a cost of $3 per order. There are hundreds of similarly specialized companies. Some have joined into pseudo-malls. They send out a CD-ROM disk each month with all their catalogs on it. The customer can browse through the disk, ask for specific assistance, or ask for more informa-

tion about a product. When an item is found that the customer wants to purchase, it can be selected. When the customer is finished selecting, the order is sent to each of the companies involved. This process will significantly reduce transaction costs for those persons who place a high value on their time. Whether catalogs or home-shopping networks displace local businesses will depend on the prices they charge for the goods they sell and the prices they charge for their services.)

EVALUATION

• Ask students to pretend that they are living during the time of their grandparents' youth. Based on what they learned in this lesson, each of them has decided to start up a new business. None of them has enough money available, but a group of outside funders is willing to help. Tell each student to write a speech that he or she will give to the funders. The presentation should include a description of the business, why this is a good business opportunity, where it will be located and why, and who the customers will be. Remind the students that when they write their speeches they should think about the information they learned in this lesson.

• Divide the students into cooperative groups and tell each group to plan a shopping center. Have them suggest the types of stores and products they would want to have in their shopping centers. Then have each member of the group choose one of the stores and write a description of the consumer base and range for this store.

EXTENSION ACTIVITY

1. Get permission for your students to survey customers at stores or business services to find out where the patrons of the stores live, so a trade area can be determined and drawn. A minimum of 30 customers should be surveyed in each case, but more would be preferable and would give a better delineation of the trade area of the store or business service. The list from Activity 1 can be used to choose stores and businesses to be surveyed.

The following questions should be asked:
• Did you come to buy a specific product or

several products?
- What product or products did you buy?
- What city or town did you come from?
- About how far did you come? (Estimate to the nearest tenth of a mile.)
- What mode of transportation did you use?
- How long did it take to get here?

Students can look up the populations of the towns represented and total them to obtain an approximation of the threshold population for each business surveyed. Based on their findings, students should write a report giving average distances and times traveled by the customers of the stores surveyed, descriptions of the products they came to buy, and the modes of transportation that they used. They should then rank the stores based on the average distance traveled by the customers of that store and compare their ranking to the ranking of Activity 1, *Where Do You Shop?*

2. Students can repeat Activity 1, *Where Do You Shop?*, asking their parents or adults within the school community to provide the necessary information. They should collect data on time and distance and compute a ranking based on each.

ACTIVITY 1
WHERE DO YOU SHOP?

Name _____

Shopping is a regular activity in most Americans' lives. Where people shop is influenced by personal knowledge, personal preferences, economic factors, and geographic factors.

You must know that a store exists before you can shop there. You may know something about the store that will discourage you from shopping there. It may be located in a high crime area, or you may know customers who were not satisfied with the products they bought there.

You may patronize a favorite restaurant because you prefer the food served there over the food at a restaurant closer to your home, or you may be attracted by the service or the personal attention you receive. Long after you have moved away from a neighborhood, you may return regularly to the shop of a favorite hairdresser or barber.

While your preferences or tastes are important influences on where you shop, your income and the prices of the goods and services you would like to purchase are even more important. In order to buy a good or service you must be able and willing to pay for it. If an identical product has a lower price at Store A than at Store B, you are likely to buy it at Store A. If a substitute product is available at a low enough price, you may buy it instead of your preferred product.

The distance you have to travel to a store is an important geographic factor. If the same quality good or service is available in two stores, and you do not have a personal preference for one store over the other, you will probably shop at the store that is closer to your home.

Assume that you have been put in charge of your family's shopping. Where would you purchase the goods and services listed in the table below? Complete the "Where purchased" column of the table. When you have finished, find the approximate location of your home on the road map and mark that location with an H. Mark the locations of each of the stores listed in the "Where purchased" column with the item number. Then measure the straight line distances that you would travel to purchase each of the items. Use the map scale to calculate how far you would travel in tenths of a mile for each product. Record the answers in the "Straight-line distance" column of the table.

Items purchased	Where purchased	Straight-line distance from home in tenths of a mile
1. Family groceries for a week		
2. Convenience store goods		
3. Primary physician		
4. Basic dental care		
5. Basic clothing (shirts, socks)		
6. Videotape rentals		
7. Haircuts or hair styling		
8. Records, tapes, or CDs		
9. Medical supplies		
10. Movie theater tickets		

From *Geography: Focus on Economics*, © National Council on Economic Education, New York, NY

ACTIVITY 2
WHERE DID YOUR GRANDPARENTS SHOP?

Name _____

To be successful, stores must locate where there are enough customers to use the stores. The choice of location involves two major geographic concepts called threshold and range. A **threshold** is the smallest number of customers necessary for a particular store to stay in business. Some businesses, such as food stores, gas stations, and taverns, can usually operate with relatively small threshold populations. Other businesses, such as professional sports teams, sometimes require threshold populations in the millions.

Range is the greatest distance people are willing to travel to purchase a good or service. Some items, such as loaves of bread, involve relatively short ranges. People don't want to travel long distances to purchase goods as common and inexpensive as bread. Other goods or services such as new automobiles might have ranges that are much larger. Purchases having long ranges are usually more expensive and are bought less frequently. The two concepts, threshold and range, are related. In order for a store to succeed, its threshold population must be within the range people are willing to travel to buy the particular good or service sold by the company.

Specialization occurs when people produce those goods and services they are most efficient at producing and trade for the other goods and services they want. The greater the number of people living in an area, the more specialization is possible. That is why you will find more specialized stores in cities while general stores are more likely to be found in rural areas. Where the population base is large enough, it will pay to build shopping malls with many specialized stores. Successful malls must have one or two major stores (called *anchors*) that have relatively large ranges. These stores will draw customers to the mall. The other stores both benefit from the presence of the major stores and provide people with more reasons for a trip to the mall.

How have shopping malls changed shopping patterns? Today, many people go on multipurpose shopping trips, often to a mall. But, 50 years ago many purchases were single-purpose shopping trips, possibly to a deli, drug store, bakery, or other store.

ASSIGNMENT

Interview three persons your grandparents' age or older. Ask them:

- What products did you buy when you were my age?

- Where did you buy them?

- How did you get to the stores?

- How old were you when you visited a shopping mall for the first time?

Based on your interviews, write a two-page summary of what shopping patterns were like 40 to 50 years ago. Include your ideas about why these patterns have changed.

VISUAL 1
WHERE WE SHOP

Student	Family Groceries	Convenience Store Goods	Physician	Dentist	Clothing	Video Rental	Hair Styling	Recorded Music	Medical Supplies	Movie Tickets
AVERAGE										
RANK										

LESSON THREE
WHY NATIONS TRADE

INTRODUCTION

Why do countries trade? Shouldn't a strong country such as the United States produce all of the computers, television sets, automobiles, cameras, and VCRs it wants rather than import such products from Japan? Why do the Japanese and other countries buy wheat, corn, chemical products, aircraft, manufactured goods, and informational services from the United States?

Because countries have different natural, human, and capital resources and different ways of combining these resources, they are not equally efficient at producing the goods and services that their residents demand. The decision to produce any good or service has an **opportunity cost,** which is the amount of another good or service that might otherwise have been produced. Given a choice of producing one good or another, it is more efficient to produce the good with the lower opportunity cost, using the increased production of that good to trade for the good with the higher opportunity cost.

When a country can produce more of a good with the same resources that another country can, it is said to have an **absolute advantage** in the production of that good. If the second country has an absolute advantage in producing a good that the first country wants, both will be better off if they specialize and trade.

But trade is usually beneficial to both countries even if one has an absolute advantage in the production of *both* goods that are to be traded. Given any two products, a nation has a **comparative advantage** in the product with the lower opportunity cost. The **terms of trade** must be such that both countries lower the opportunity costs of the goods they are getting from the trade.

Why do countries have different opportunity costs? They have different endowments of productive resources—warmer climates and longer growing seasons; more plentiful natural resources such as oil, iron ore, and water; more highly educated and skilled workers; and larger quantities of more sophisticated machinery.

World trade is not static. It has been increasing both in amount and in significance. New supplies of natural resources can be discovered and developed while existing supplies are better managed. Human resources can be improved through better educational programs. Capital resources can be acquired to make the better trained workers even more productive. The increase in world trade should result in more efficient use of the world's scarce resources, and in higher standards of living.

CONCEPTS

Opportunity Cost
Absolute Advantage
Comparative Advantage
Specialization
Terms of Trade

OBJECTIVES

◆ Recognize that comparative advantage is the basis for trade.

◆ Engage in a comparative advantage simulation.

◆ Analyze the simulation results and use the comparative advantage model to make a decision about specialization.

◆ Predict the consequences of one's decisions.

LESSON DESCRIPTION

Students read and discuss a narrative about international trade that focuses on opportunity cost and the principle of comparative advantage. Then the class is divided into four groups, each representing a different country. They engage in a simulation that assesses the skills available within their countries, and each country decides on an area of specialization. The lesson ends with a class discussion about the decisions made by the four countries and the economic benefits and/or costs of those decisions.

TIME REQUIRED

Three class periods. (Two if the reading of Activity 1, *Comparative Advantage,* is assigned as homework.)

MATERIALS

■ One copy for each student of Activity 1, *Comparative Advantage*

★ One copy for each student of Activity 2, *Human Resources and Comparative Advantage*. Several copies of Activity 3, *Bureaucratic Skills Test* (one with the answers for the tester.) Several copies of Activity 4, *Computer Skills Test* (one with the answers for the tester.)

PROCEDURE

PERIOD 1

1. Distribute Activity 1, *Comparative Advantage*. Allow students sufficient time to read the explanation of comparative advantage or assign the reading for homework. (This is a difficult concept for students at all levels to understand. You may choose to treat the activity as a text and read through it step by step with your students. Once you think the students understand the concept, use steps 2 through 9 as a review.)

2. Copy TABLE A on the board. Ask the following questions:

   • What would be the total production of shoes and shirts without specialization and trade? (180 units of shoes and 175 units of shirts.)

   • How many units of each good would the United States have? (100 units of shoes and 75 units of shirts.)

   • How many units of each good would Canada have? (80 units of shoes and 100 units of shirts.)

3. Copy TABLE B on the board. Ask the following questions:

   • How did specialization affect world production? (Added 20 units of shoes and 25 units of shirts.)

   • How did specialization and trade affect the standard of living in the United States? In Canada? (The United States added 25 units of shirts. Canada added 20 units of shoes.)

4. Copy TABLE C on the board. Ask the following questions:

   • What would be the total production of shoes and shirts without specialization and trade? (180 units of shoes and 155 units of shirts.)

   • How many units of each good would the United States have? (100 units of shoes and 80 units of shirts.)

   • How many units of each good would Canada have? (80 units of shoes and 75 units of shirts.)

5. Copy TABLE D on the board. Ask the following questions:

   • How did specialization affect world production? (Added 20 units of shoes and lost 5 units of shirts.)

6. Copy TABLE E on the board. Ask the following questions:

   • How did this case of partial specialization increase total production from TABLE C? (Added 10 units of shoes and 3 units of shirts.)

   • Assume that the United States trades 85 units of shoes to Canada for 75 units of shirts as shown below:

	Shoes	Shirts
United States	105	83
Canada	85	75
Total	190	158

   How many units of each good would the United States have? (105 units of shoes and 83 units of shirts.)

   • How many units of each good would Canada have? (85 units of shoes and 75 units of shirts.)

   • Would this be an improvement over TABLE C? (The United States would add 5 units of shoes and 3 units of shirts; Canada would add 5 units of shoes.)

★ all students–basic course material
■ average and above average students
○ average and below average students

7. Suppose that the United States trades 90 units of shoes to Canada for 75 units of shirts as shown below. Would both countries be better off than in TABLE C? (The United States would add 3 units of shirts and Canada would add 10 units of shoes.)

	Shoes	Shirts
United States	100	83
Canada	90	75
Total	190	158

8. Why wouldn't the United States trade 95 units of shoes for 75 units of shirts?

	Shoes	Shirts
United States	95	83
Canada	95	75
Total	190	158

(Without specialization the United States had 100 units of shoes and 80 units of shirts. The opportunity cost of one unit of shirts was 1.25 units of shoes. Three shirts would cost 3.75 units shoes. This trade would give up 5 units of shoes for 3 shirts.)

9. Who benefits when countries trade? (Both countries benefit or no trade will take place.)

PERIOD 2

10. Set up the classroom as described in Activity 2, *Human Resources and Comparative Advantage.* (Corner #1, SERVICE SKILLS; Corner #2, SALES SKILLS; Corner #3, BUREAUCRATIC SKILLS; Corner #4, COMPUTER SKILLS; Center of the Classroom, OTHER.)

11. Provide someone to administer the tests in Corner #3 (Activity 3, *Bureaucratic Skills Test*) and Corner #4 (Activity 4, *Computer Skills Test*).

12. Divide the remaining students into 4 approximately equal groups. Explain to the students that they should not be discouraged if they find one or more of the tests from Activity 2 to be difficult. If everyone got all the questions right, there would be no reason to specialize, and this activity is about specialization based on comparative advantage.

13. Distribute Activity 2, *Human Resources and Comparative Advantage.* Have the groups meet, read over the activity, and decide what they have to do. Once they have indicated they are ready to begin their testing, signal them to begin. After 10, 20, and 30 minutes, remind them to move to another testing area; after 40 minutes, have them regroup in their countries to complete steps 4 through 7 of Activity 2.

Answers for Activity 3:
1. ½ point for each word in correct position.
   synecdoche
   synecious
   synecology
   synectics
   synergist
   synergy
   synesis
   synesthesia
2. 2 points for each correct answer.
   a. Yes   b. Yes   c. No

Answers for Activity 4:
One point for each correct answer.
1. (28 days)
2. (11010)
3. (1000)
4. (7)
5. (Jane, 3, Jonas, 9, Juan)
6. (.202)
7. (7)
8. (3)
9. (10)
10. (100, 4, 4, 40)

14. Put the chart under step 8 of Activity 2 on the board. Have each country fill in its information. Ask each country what it decided to produce and the reasoning behind the decision.

CLOSURE
- Have each student make a copy of the completed chart under step 8 of Activity 2.

- Ask each student to write a one-page paper explaining why their country should or should not specialize and trade. They must discuss the opportunity costs involved and how comparative advantage has influenced their decision. They should mention likely trading partners in their explanation.

EVALUATION

- Ask the students to write an original paragraph about two fictional countries and the products that they might exchange. Tell them to be sure to explain why these countries chose to produce these products, and what kind of trade will take place between these countries.

- Ask your most able students to define *Absolute Advantage* and *Comparative Advantage* and to explain how the two are different.

EXTENSION

1. Ask each student to look for newspaper and periodical articles that discuss international trade. Have a committee of students develop a clipping file on such topics as NAFTA, Mexico's peso crisis, the impact of rising interest rates in the United States on investment in developing countries such as Mexico, the impact of middle-class Mexicans buying U.S.-made consumer goods, major trading partners of the United States, U.S. trade relations with Japan and other Pacific Rim countries, the return of Hong Kong to China, U.S. trade relations with Canada, GATT, widening NAFTA to include Latin American countries, U.S. trade relations with Russia and the other former Soviet states, and U.S. trade relations with the European Economic Community. (Give students credit for contributing to or organizing the file.)

2. Allow students to write short (one page) summaries of articles from the clipping file with at least one additional paragraph explaining how opportunity cost and comparative advantage help them to understand what is going on in the situation described in the article. (Students who submit thoughtful and perceptive analyses should be encouraged to report their papers to the class.)

ACTIVITY 1
COMPARATIVE ADVANTAGE

Name_____

The reading for this lesson explains why countries trade with each other. Even when countries can produce what they want on their own, they often choose to specialize. They import some things and export others. People specialize for the same reasons that countries specialize. As you read this explanation, think about the following questions:

1. Why do countries choose to specialize and trade?

2. When might they choose not to?

3. How does comparative advantage apply to you?

4. How can you choose a lifestyle that encourages you to do what you do best?

ABSOLUTE ADVANTAGE

Pretend for a moment that there are just two countries in the world, the United States and Canada. Pretend also that they produce only two goods, shoes and shirts. The resources of both countries can be used to produce either shoes or shirts. Both countries make both products, spending half of their working hours on each. But the United States makes more shoes than shirts, and Canada makes more shirts than shoes. This situation is shown in Table A.

TABLE A

	Shoes	Shirts
United States	100	75
Canada	80	100
Total	180	175

Now, the sensible thing to do would be for each country to specialize. The United States should make only shoes and Canada should make only shirts. What will happen when each country spends all its working hours making one product? It will make twice as much of that product and none of the other, as shown in Table B.

TABLE B

	Shoes	Shirts
United States	200	0
Canada	0	200
Total	200	200

The world now has both more shoes and more shirts. The United States can trade 100 units of shoes for 100 units of shirts, and both countries will benefit.

In this example, the United States could make more shoes than Canada with the same resources. Economists say that it had an *absolute advantage* at shoemaking. Canada, on the other hand, had an *absolute advantage* at shirtmaking.

COMPARATIVE ADVANTAGE

Now suppose one country has an absolute advantage in both products. Is trade a good idea under these circumstances? Table C shows what production might be like if the United States had an absolute advantage at making both shoes and shirts.

TABLE C

	Shoes	Shirts
United States	100	80
Canada	80	75
Total	180	155

In this case, the United States can produce more of each good with the same set of resources than Canada can. The **opportunity cost** of choosing to produce more of one of the goods with the available resources will be the loss of some of the other good. The United States could produce either 200 units of shoes or 160 units of shirts. Canada could produce either 160 units of shoes or 150 units of shirts. If the United States produces only shoes, it gives up 80 units of shirts to gain 100 units of shoes. If Canada produces only

ACTIVITY 1 (continued)

shoes, it gives up 75 units of shirts to gain 80 units of shoes. The opportunity cost of producing shirts is higher for the United States, and the opportunity cost of producing shoes is lower. The opportunity cost of producing shoes is higher for Canada, and the opportunity cost of producing shirts is lower. Economists would say that the United States has a *comparative advantage* in shoemaking and Canada has a *comparative advantage* in shirtmaking. Table D shows what happens when each country specializes in the product in which it has a comparative advantage.

TABLE D

	Shoes	Shirts
United States	200	0
Canada	0	150
Total	200	150

By specializing in this way, the United States and Canada have increased the production of shoes by twenty units over what they produced before, from 180 to 200. But the world has lost five units of shirts, going from 155 to 150. (See Table C.) Production in the United States could be adjusted to make up the difference. For example, if the United States gave up 10 units of shoes, it could produce 8 units of shirts. Table E shows the results of such a tradeoff.

TABLE E

	Shoes	Shirts
United States	190	8
Canada	0	150
Total	190	158

In this way, the total production of both goods could be increased.

TERMS OF TRADE

What will be the **terms of trade** in this situation? Before specialization the United States produced 100 fewer units of shoes. The opportunity cost of choosing to produce 80 units of shirts was the 100 units of shoes that could have been produced with the same resources. In like manner, Canada's opportunity cost of producing 80 units of shoes was 75 units of shirts. If the terms of trade reduce each country's opportunity cost of acquiring the good traded for, trade will take place. In this example, Canada will not accept fewer than 80 units of shoes for 75 units of shirts and the United States will not pay more than 100 units of shoes for 80 units of shirts. Both countries must benefit for trade to occur.

The real world is much more complex than this two-country, two-product model. Trade involves many different countries and products. And it is not always clear where a country's comparative advantage lies.

ACTIVITY 2
HUMAN RESOURCES AND COMPARATIVE ADVANTAGE

Name _____

Comparative advantage can be applied to people as well as to countries. It says, in effect, that it is best for everyone when people concentrate on doing the one thing they do best. If fixing things is your specialty, for instance, that is what you should do. It doesn't matter that other people may be better at fixing things than you are. But if you are also an artist, you may have to decide which of your two skills is your comparative advantage. This will depend in part on other people's strengths and the value that society places on your skills. You must ask yourself which of the things you can produce is worth more in trade. This activity shows how the skills of a country's residents help to define its comparative advantage.

Comparative advantage is a difficult concept to understand. Pretend for this activity that it is possible to predict the future accurately, that the tests really measure your skills, and that wages in the four skill areas are about the same. (Don't be discouraged if some of the tests seem hard compared to the others. The activity won't work if everyone has a perfect score on each test.)

1. You have been divided into four groups. Each group represents a country whose goal is to decide which of its resources should be developed for trade. Your own abilities, which will be tested in this activity, are the resources your country can choose to develop.

2. Economists predict four skill areas that will be in great demand for the next twenty years. The skills are service skills, sales skills, computer skills, and bureaucratic skills. Your country will determine which it should focus on by having all of its citizens tested for their ability in each of the four skill areas.

Each corner of the classroom should be designated as the testing center for determining ability in one of the four skill areas. There will be four ten-minute testing sessions timed by the teacher. This will insure that you have enough time to go to all four corners to be tested in all four skill areas. If you finish any test early, you may move on to the next corner. Instructions explaining how the tests are to be administered follow.

Corner #1   SERVICE SKILLS
- Your service ability will be measured by what kind of person you seem to be.
- Introduce yourself to someone else in the corner and convince that person that you can be trusted.
- This person must decide how much confidence she or he has in you and, consequently, how much you might be able to help her or him. She or he will rate you on a scale of 1 to 10, 10 being the highest grade possible.

Corner #2   SALES SKILLS
- Your sales ability is measured by how effective a one-minute sales pitch you can come up with is.
- Go up to one person in this corner and give her or him a one-minute sales talk on a product she or he has randomly chosen.
- This person will rate your sales ability on a scale of 1 to 10 by deciding your effectiveness in convincing her or him to buy your product.

Corner #3   BUREAUCRATIC SKILLS
- Your ability to work in a bureaucracy is measured by how well you can alphabetize eight words and apply a rule to three cases.
- The teacher or a student volunteer acts as tester in this corner. The tester gives a copy of the test to you and corrects it when you have finished.
- You will receive a half point for each word alphabetized correctly and two points for each question correctly answered.

From *Geography: Focus on Economics*, © National Council on Economic Education, New York, NY

ACTIVITY 1 (continued)

Corner #4 COMPUTER SKILLS
- Your computer ability is measured by how well you perform on a mathematics test.
- A teacher or student volunteer will have to administer this test.
- You will receive one point for every correct answer.

Center of the Classroom

You must take at least two of the skills tests. If you decide not to take the others, you can spend the testing session in the center of the classroom. While there, you must create your own job category, test, and rating scale.

4. After you have taken four ability tests, meet with the other members of your country. Everyone should fill in the following ability score chart on a separate piece of paper and drop it into a hat or box. Charts can remain nameless. If you did not take a certain test, then you should write in a 0 as your score.

	YOUR ABILITY SCORE
Service	
Sales	
Computer	
Bureaucratic	
Other	

5. Your country must now compute a productivity score for each of its potential resources by adding up the individual scores for each resource.

It is not necessary to include alternative service scores unless the scores are particularly significant. Complete the following chart or copy the chart on a separate sheet of paper.

	YOUR COUNTRY'S PRODUCTIVITY SCORE
Service	
Sales	
Computer	
Bureaucratic	
Other	

6. Based on its productivity scores, decide what would be best for your country to concentrate on developing.

7. Discussion questions for each country to ask itself:

- Should you do only what you do better than anybody else, following your absolute advantage?
- Should you do only what you can do best, following your comparative advantage?
- Should you try to be self-sufficient, producing everything?

8. All four countries should next decide what it would be best for each country to produce. Copy the following comparative advantage chart on the board and fill in the necessary information.

	PRODUCTIVITY SCORES			
	COUNTRY A	COUNTRY B	COUNTRY C	COUNTRY D
Service				
Sales				
Computer				
Bureaucratic				
Other				

ACTIVITY 3
BUREAUCRATIC SKILLS TEST

Name _____

1. Put the following eight words in alphabetical order:

   synesthesia   _____
   synecdoche   _____
   synergist   _____
   synetics   _____
   synergy   _____
   synesis   _____
   synecious   _____
   synecology   _____

2. The following is a National Park Service rule:

   "No person shall prune, cut, carry away, pull up, dig, fell, bore, chop, saw, chip, pick, move, sever, climb, molest, take, break, deface, destroy, set fire to, burn, scorch, carve, paint, mark, or in any manner interfere with, tamper, mutilate, misuse, disturb, or damage any tree, shrub, plant, grass, flower, or any part thereof, nor shall any person permit any chemical, whether solid, fluid, or gaseous, to seep, drip, drain, or be emptied, sprayed, dusted on, injected upon, about or into any tree, shrub, plant, grass, flower."

   According to the rule, are these actions permissible?

   a. mutilate a tree in your back yard

   b. collect firewood in a national park

   c. carve your initials on the bark of a small shrub in a national forest

 From *Geography: Focus on Economics*, © National Council on Economic Education, New York, NY

ACTIVITY 4
COMPUTER SKILLS TEST

Name _____

1. If a kangaroo at the bottom of a 30-foot well jumps up three feet every day and slides back two feet, how long will it take her to reach the top? (days)

2. Convert 26 (base l0) to base 2.   (   )

3. 100101 (base 2) minus 11101 (base 2) = ?

4. $(2.5 \times 10^4) \times (4.0 \times 10^2) = I \times 10^{(?)}$ (   )

5. If Jonas is six inches taller than Juan and Jonas is three inches shorter than Jane, then the tallest person is __?__, who is __?__ inches taller than ___?___ and __?__ inches taller than __?__.

6. 4.6864 divided by 23.2 = ?

7. 28 is __?__ % of 400.

8. If $4(x–2) + 7y + 3 = 21$ and $y = 2$, then x= ?

9. Find the average of the following numbers: 1,3,7,10,13,17,and 19.   (   )

10. Sue works 40 hours a week and earns $4 an hour. For every dollar she earns, she pays five cents in taxes. She can calculate her take-home pay in dollars by: Dividing 5 by __?__ , multiplying the answer by __?__ , subtracting that answer from __?__ , and then multiplying by __?__ .

LESSON FOUR
INTERNATIONAL INTERDEPENDENCE

INTRODUCTION

International trade happens because of decisions of individuals, businesses, and government agencies to buy goods and services produced in other nations or to sell goods and services to individuals, businesses, and government agencies in other nations. The United States is a major participant in the global economy.

The United States is the world's largest trading nation, providing 12 to 15% of the goods and services that other nations purchase. The United States is not as dependent on international trade as some other countries because of its large, diversified resource base, and important internal markets. For example, if California were a country, it would be the world's 10th largest economy. But U.S. exports and imports have risen from a total of 9.4% of real Gross Domestic Product (real GDP) in 1960 to 24.8% in 1993 and may reach 40% within the present decade. (**Gross Domestic Product** is the total market value, expressed in dollars, of all final goods and services produced in an economy. **Real GDP** is GDP adjusted for price changes.) Our nearest neighbors, Canada and Mexico, depend on the United States to provide them with imports and to purchase their exports.

Trade in the services used by complex technological economies, is an expanding part of the United States' international activity. These are called **invisible exports**. Most of U.S. trade will probably continue to be with developed countries.

CONCEPTS
International Trade
Gross Domestic Product
Real Gross Domestic Product
Exports
Imports
Interdependence
Visible Exports

Invisible Exports
Opportunity Cost

OBJECTIVES
◆ Utilize data from tables and graphs to answer questions.

◆ Analyze data about the United States' role in international trade.

◆ Hypothesize about the United States' role in international trade based on the data.

◆ Construct a written argument in support of the hypothesis.

LESSON DESCRIPTION
Students provide information about foreign-made goods that they and their families have purchased, and a master list is compiled. Then they hypothesize reasons why people buy goods made in other countries, and these reasons are also recorded. They are asked whether foreign trade is more important, less important, or equally important to the United States and other countries, and their answers are recorded.

Following an activity, which gives them an intensive look at graphical data concerning international trade, the students reconsider their earlier answers and discuss the importance of international trade for the United States.

TIME REQUIRED
Three class periods.

MATERIALS
■ A copy of Activity 1, *The Importance of International Trade to the United States* for each student.
○ A copy of Activity 2, *The Importance of the United States to International Trade* for each student.
★ A copy of Activity 3, *United States' Trading Partners* for each student.

PROCEDURE
1. Explain that this lesson is about the United States' role in the global economy. Explain that you want to compile a list of products that the stu-

★ all students–basic course material
■ average and above average students
○ average and below average students

dents and their families have purchased that were made outside the United States. Ask the students to take out a piece of paper and to write down 10 such items. (If your students need more time to compile their lists, you might want to ask them to do it as a homework assignment the evening before you begin the lesson. They can check such things as labels on clothes and food packages, and get help from adults at home.)

2. After allowing a few minutes, ask each student to read her or his list aloud. Compile a master list on the board. Place a check mark next to an item each time it is repeated. (Possible answers include coffee, tea, cocoa, bananas, spices, cars, televisions, radios, video recorders, computers, clothing, and athletic shoes.) Remind the students that American businesses also buy overseas, and that resources such as foreign oil play an important role in the American economy.

3. When the list has filled the board, ask the students to write down why we buy goods produced in other countries. Compile a list of these answers. (Students may say that the products aren't produced in the United States, that the foreign-made products are better quality, or that the foreign-made products are less expensive than their American-made counterparts. If you have used Lesson 3, someone may say that the foreign producers of these products have a comparative advantage over their American competitors.)

4. Ask the students to think about how important foreign trade is to the United States economy. Tell them to write on their papers the word "more" if they think it is more important to the United States than it is to other countries, the word "less" if it is less important to the United States than it is to other countries, and the word "same" if it is about as important to the United States as it is to other countries. Then ask for a show of hands for each response and record the number of hands raised each time.

5. Distribute Activity 1, *The Importance of International Trade to the United States,* and allow students enough time to read it and answer the questions. When the students have finished the activity, discuss the answers and clear up any misunderstandings. The students may not be able to read the exact values from the chart, so accept approximate answers as being close enough and tell the students what the exact values are.

Answers for Activity 1:
1. 4.5%
2. 4.9%
3. 9.4%
4. 13.2%
5. 11.6%
6. 24.8%
7. More Important

6. Distribute Activity 2, *The Importance of the United States to International Trade,* and allow students enough time to read it and answer the questions. Discuss the answers.

Possible Answers for Activity 2:

Visible Exports		Invisible Exports	
corn	$5.7 billion	legal services	$1.4 billion
peanuts	$0.21 billion	financial services	$5.4 billion
passenger craft	$24.5 billion	education services	$6.1 billion
wheat	$4.6 billion	passenger fares	$17.4 billion
aluminum	$1.2 billion	management consulting services	$0.78 billion
vegetable oils	$1.0 billion	information services	$2.6 billion

7. Distribute Activity 3, *United States' Trading Partners,* and allow students enough time to read it and answer the questions. Discuss the answers.

Answers for Activity 3:
1. 64.8%
2. 68.7%
3. 8
4. Canada, Japan, and Mexico
5. 39.8%, and 43.4%
6. U.S. imports have been greater than exports for most of the years. Because the Chart 1 graph uses five year intervals, it is not possible to be more specific.

Note: Activity 1, *The Importance of International Trade to the United States*, Activity 2, *The Importance of the United States to International Trade*, and Activity 3, *United States' Trading Partners*, can be assigned as homework and then discussed in class. This procedure will give less able students enough time to think about the questions and get help if needed.

CLOSURE

- Ask the students to review Activity 1 and write a sentence that describes the importance of international trade to the United States.

- Ask the students to review Activity 2 and write a sentence that describes the importance of the United States to international trade.

- Ask selected students to read their sentences.

EVALUATION

- Ask the students to recall the fictional countries and products that they created in Lesson 3. Tell them to make a list of both the visible exports and a list of invisible exports that each country might be selling.

- Ask the students to pretend that they are running for Congress. Tell them to prepare a television speech or a newspaper ad that will explain their position on international trade. Tell them to include information they have learned in this lesson in their statement.

EXTENSION

1. Students can locate the countries which are the 10 top purchasers of United States' exports on a world map. They can locate the countries that are the 10 top suppliers of United States' imports on a similar map. More ambitious students can construct choropleth maps based on the dollar amount of the exports or imports or based on the percentages of the exports or imports. (If the students have not worked with choropleth maps, they can use the directions from Lesson 7, Activity 2.)

2. Present the following statement that Adam Smith wrote in *The Wealth of Nations* in 1776:

> What is prudence in the conduct of every private family, can scarce be folly in that of a great kingdom. If a foreign country can supply us with a commodity cheaper than we ourselves can make it, better buy it of them with some part of the produce

of our own industry, employed in a way in which we have some advantage.

Ask the students whether Smith is in favor of or against international trade. Ask the students to summarize Smith's position in a paragraph.

ACTIVITY 1
THE IMPORTANCE OF INTERNATIONAL TRADE TO THE UNITED STATES

Name _____

When we talk about trade between countries, we are talking about the exchange of goods and services between people, businesses, and government agencies in those countries. Goods and services produced in one country but sold to buyers in another country are called **exports**. Goods and services bought from sellers in another country are **imports**.

The amount of world trade has been increasing. Countries are trading more and that trade is increasing compared to what they produce at home. The more countries trade with one another, the more **interdependent** they become. The United States is almost wholly dependent on other countries for some of the products it consumes daily. We all know people who would have great difficulty surviving a day without coffee, tea, or chocolate. Life would not be as pleasant without bananas for our cereal, spices for our cooking, and music from our portable tape players. Could we survive without these imports? Of course we could, and at times we have. We trade because the goods and services that we give up when we trade, called our **opportunity costs**, are less valuable to us than the goods and services we get by trading.

Some businesses in the United States depend on selling goods and services in foreign markets. Large amounts of chemicals, aircraft, cars, computers, and agricultural products such as wheat and cotton are sold to foreign buyers.

How important are imports and exports to the U.S. economy? Chart 1 provides information that may help us tackle this question. It shows United States Exports and Imports as a percent of Real Gross Domestic Product. **Gross Domestic Product** is the total market value, expressed in dollars, of all final goods and services produced in an economy. **Real Gross Domestic Product** (real GDP) is adjusted for price changes, allowing comparisons to be made over the years. As a way of understanding what information this chart contains, answer the following questions (While you won't be able to read the exact value from the graph, answer as accurately as you can.):

1. U.S.exports were what percent of Real GDP in 1960? _____

2. Imports were what percent of Real GDP in 1960? _____

3. Trade (exports plus imports) with other nations was what percent of Real GDP in 1960? _____

4. Imports were what percent of Real GDP in 1993? _____

5. Exports were what percent of Real GDP in 1993? _____

6. trade (exports plus imports) with other nations was what percent of Real GDP in 1993? _____

7. Based on this chart, would you say that international trade was becoming more important, less important, or staying about the same for the United States? _____

ACTIVITY 1 (continued)

U.S. Trade as Share of Real Gross Domestic Product

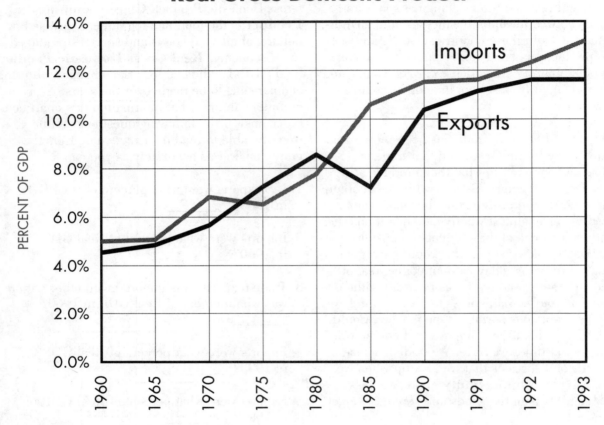

Imports

Exports

PERCENT OF GDP

14.0%
12.0%
10.0%
8.0%
6.0%
4.0%
2.0%
0.0%

1960 1965 1970 1975 1980 1985 1990 1991 1992 1993

Source: *Economic Report of the President,* 1994, pp. 270–71

From *Geography: Focus on Economics,* © National Council on Economic Education, New York, NY

ACTIVITY 2
THE IMPORTANCE OF THE UNITED STATES TO INTERNATIONAL TRADE

Name _____

The United States is the world's largest trading nation. The United States provides between 12 and 15% of the world's exports. In addition to **visible exports,** goods that can be counted, the United States is the world's largest provider of **invisible exports** which are services. Shipping, travel and tourism, insurance, banking, advertising, and education are examples of these services. They are called invisible exports because it is so much more difficult to measure them. Table 1 describes some of our most important visible and invisible exports.

Table 1

U.S. Exports: More Than Peanuts

In 1992, American service firms exported:

- over two-thirds as much in passenger fares ($17.4 billion) on U.S. airplanes as the value of United States passenger aircraft sold ($24.5 billion)
- more educational services ($6.1 billion) than corn ($5.7 billion)
- more financial services ($5.4 billion) than wheat ($4.6 billion)
- more equipment installation and repair services ($2.8 billion) than farm machinery ($2.1 billion)
- more information services, including computer and data processing ($2.6 billion) than aluminum ($1.2 billion)
- more legal services ($1.4 billion) than vegetable oils ($1.0 billion)
- more management consulting services ($0.78 billion) than milled rice ($0.72 billion) or peanuts ($0.21 billion).

Source: *Economic Report of the President*, 1994, p. 209.

To see if you understand the difference between visible exports and invisible exports, complete the chart below by adding 5 visible and 5 invisible exports.

Visible Exports		Invisible Exports	
corn	$5.7 billion	legal services	$1.4 billion

Summary: The United States depends on other countries to provide imports that we cannot produce as efficiently ourselves. The United States depends on other countries to buy exports that we produce more efficiently than they do. International trade is growing in importance for nations throughout the world and for the United States. While the United States is not as dependent on international trade as many other countries, the United States is the world's largest trading nation. More and more of this trade is in services, which are called invisible exports.

ACTIVITY 3
UNITED STATES' TRADING PARTNERS

Name _____

   With whom does the United States trade? Most of our import and export trade is with developed countries like ourselves, not with the less developed countries or the countries of eastern Europe. Table 2 shows the 10 top purchasers of U.S. Merchandise Exports. These countries bought $289.9 billion worth of our $448.2 billion of merchandise exports. Table 3 shows the 10 top suppliers of imports to the United States. These countries provided $365.6 billion of our $532.5 billion of merchandise imports. Use these tables to answer the following questions:

1. What percent of U.S. exports were purchased by the top 10 countries? _____

2. What percent of U.S. imports were supplied by the top 10 countries? _____

3. How many countries are on both lists as top 10 buyers of exports and top ten suppliers of imports? _____

4. The United States' top three trading partners are _____, _____, and _____.

5. Together these countries buy _____ percent of our exports and supply _____ percent of our imports.

6. Using Tables 2 and 3, and the chart from Activity 1, *The Importance of International Trade to the United States*, what is the current relationship between U.S. imports and exports, and what has the relationship been like over the past 30 years?

   _____

   _____

ACTIVITY 3 (continued)

Table 2

	The Top Purchasers of U.S. Merchandise Exports in 1992		
Rank	**Country**	**Millions of Dollars**	**Percent of Total**
1	Canada	90,562	20.2%
2	Japan	47,764	10.6%
3	Mexico	40,598	9.0%
4	United Kingdom	22,808	5.1%
5	Germany	21,236	4.7%
6	Taiwan	15,205	3.4%
7	South Korea	14,630	3.3%
8	France	14,575	3.2%
9	Netherlands	13,740	3.1%
10	Belgium	9,779	2.2%
	Rest of the World	158,259	35.2%

Source: Statistical Abstract of the United States, 1993, Table No. 1351

Table 3

	The Top Suppliers of U.S. Merchandise Imports in 1992		
Rank	**Country**	**Millions of Dollars**	**Percent of Total**
1	Canada	98,497	18.5%
2	Japan	97,181	18.3%
3	Mexico	35,189	6.6%
4	Germany	28,829	5.4%
5	Taiwan	23,023	4.3%
6	United Kingdom	20,152	3.8%
7	China	18,969	3.6%
8	South Korea	16,691	3.1%
9	France	14,811	2.8%
10	Italy	12,300	2.3%
	Rest of the World	166,856	31.3%

Source: Statistical Abstract of the United States, 1993, Table No. 1351

LESSON FIVE
MONEY AROUND THE WORLD

INTRODUCTION

Money contributes to the smooth operation of an economy. Without money, individuals would have to barter to obtain the goods and services they want. The amount of money in circulation in an economy affects the nominal prices of goods and services but not their relative prices. If the amount of money were to double without any change in the goods and services available, and the demand for these goods and services didn't change, prices for all goods and services should double. It is the nominal prices, the number of units of currency, that would double. The relative prices, the prices of each product compared to the prices of the other products, would not change. For example, if the dollar price of products doubled and one product went from $1 to $2 while a second product went from 25 cents to 50 cents, the first product would still cost four times as much as the second product.

Different currencies are used in different countries. Extensive international trade requires an organized system for exchanging money between nations. An **exchange rate** is the price of one nation's currency in terms of another nation's currency. A change in exchange rates can have a significant effect on the flow of trade between nations and on a nation's domestic economy. When the exchange rate between currencies changes, it changes the relative prices of goods and services traded by the two countries. In the long run, exchange rates should adjust so that the purchasing power of a nation's money should be the same worldwide. If a market basket of goods and services costs $100 in the United States and $125 (Canadian) in Canada, the exchange rate should be one American dollar equals 1.25 Canadian dollars. Exchange rates will insure that a dollar spent in Japan, England, France, or Mexico should have approximately equal purchasing power.

CONCEPTS
Money
Prices
Exchange Rates
Foreign Exchange Markets
Demand
Supply

OBJECTIVES

◆ Participate in two or three auctions.

◆ Recognize the role that money plays in domestic trade.

◆ Calculate prices of U.S. goods in foreign currencies.

◆ Describe the role that foreign exchange markets play in facilitating exports and imports.

◆ Analyze the similarities and differences between the auctions and the foreign exchange activity.

LESSON DESCRIPTION

Students participate in one of two class auctions so that they may experience firsthand how prices are determined in different markets. The class is divided into two groups. Members of each group are given either macaroni or bean money which they use to bid for items, using only their group's designated money. Final sale prices are recorded and compared for each group's auction. Students discuss the reasons why prices differed for the two groups.

A second set of auctions is conducted, but this time students are allowed to trade money and participate in both auctions. They discuss the results of the auctions and the average rate of exchange between the two forms of money.

Students then participate in a foreign exchange activity, determining the prices of a bundle of American-made goods in Japanese yen, Canadian dollars, and British pounds during two time periods. They hypothesize reasons for the changes they observe.

TIME REQUIRED
Two to three class periods.

MATERIALS

★ One copy of Activity 1, *Money Markets*, for each student or group of students.
Packages of two or four of the following for use as currencies: macaroni, beans, cereal, paper clips, jelly beans, or similar items.

★ Four copies of Activity 2, *Country A Goods*, and Activity 3, *Country B Goods*. You will need to personalize these activities for your students with the names of their favorite athletes, holidays, colleges, tapes and compact discs, movies, and comics.
Calculators (optional).

PROCEDURE

AUCTION ONE

1. Explain that the class will be participating in auctions in order to better understand how money and prices are related through markets.

2. Divide the class into two groups of approximately the same number of students. Separate the two groups and tell them that they are residents of two neighboring countries that do not permit their citizens to trade with one another. Once a year in each of the countries, people receive their income. Then there is an auction of the goods that have been produced.

3. Distribute a number of pieces of macaroni to each of the students in Country A. (Give each student five to 15 pieces in a random pattern with an average of 10 pieces per student.) Then distribute beans in the same way to each of the students in Country B, but distribute three to seven beans with an average of five beans per student. The total amount of *macaroni money* will be twice the total amount of the *bean money*.

4. Cut up two copies of Activity 2, *Country A Goods*, and two copies of Activity 3, *Country B Goods*, to obtain the goods to be auctioned. Put lists of the goods to be auctioned on the board. Note that only the last three items on each list are different.

Country A Goods: football cards, hockey cards, basketball cards, baseball cards, milk, orange juice, apples, ballpoint pens, holiday pencils, music tapes, compact discs, bananas, movie posters, greeting cards, colored pencils, colored markers, movie passes, video rentals, rubber stamps, college T-shirts, comic books.

Country B Goods: football cards, hockey cards, basketball cards, baseball cards, milk, orange juice, apples, ballpoint pens, holiday pencils, music tapes, compact discs, bananas, movie posters, greeting cards, colored pencils, colored markers, movie passes, video rentals, rulers, college caps, stuffed animals.

5. Auction items one by one for Country A, recording the sale prices (in macaroni) for each on the board. Repeat the auction process for Country B, recording prices (in beans) in a separate list on the board.

6. Ask the students why macaroni prices were generally higher than bean prices. (Macaroni money was more abundant than bean money, but the quantities of goods available was about the same, so people were able to bid higher in the country with macaroni money. Since some of the goods available in one country were not available in the other, we can't rely entirely on money differences to explain the higher prices. If the prices in macaroni money were not generally higher than prices in bean money, ask how many students have money they have not spent. It may be that everyone wanted to bid for the items that were available for bean money but not for macaroni money, but nobody wanted to bid on, or bid very much, for the items that were available for macaroni money but not for bean money.)

7. Collect any money that has not been spent.

AUCTION TWO

8. Divide the class into the same two groups as in Auction One.

9. Distribute the macaroni and bean money as in Step 3. If some students have *saved* money from Auction One, use different kinds of money.

10. Prepare the goods to be auctioned and put the lists of the goods to be auctioned on the board as in Step 4. Tell the students that the governments of the two countries have decided to permit international trade.

★ all students–basic course material
■ average and above average students
○ average and below average students

39

11. Tell the class that anyone who wants to bid on the goods produced in the other country must pay for their purchases in the money of that country. Tell them that they will have 15 minutes, during which time they may trade money. Each time a trade is made they must submit a record of the transaction, using the approved format. The person who offers to make the trade should be listed as the seller. Copy this form on the board:

	(Student Name)
Sold	(Number of units of money)
To	(Student Name)
For	(Number of units of money)

12. Auction items one by one for Country A, allowing anyone with the proper money to bid. Record the sale prices (in macaroni or the money in use in that country) for each on the board. Repeat the auction process for Country B, recording prices (in beans or the money in use in that country) in a separate list on the board.

13. Discuss the results of the two auctions. (The sales prices in macaroni money should still be higher than those in bean money. The prices in both countries may have increased from the first set of auctions if students who were not interested in the goods available in their country did not participate in those auctions. Allowing trading of money should have increased the number of bidders and the size of their bids.)

14. Using the money transaction records, compute an average exchange rate. (Total the number of units of macaroni traded, total the number of units of bean money traded, and divide the first total by the second total to get the average number of units of macaroni money exchanged for a unit of bean money. It should approximate two units of macaroni money for one unit of bean money.)

15. Close this class by asking the students:

- What role did money play in the first set of auctions? (It allowed the people in each country to buy goods and services produced in their country.)

- What additional role did money play in the second set of auctions? (It allowed the people to buy goods and services produced in both countries by providing a foreign exchange market.)

- How were prices of goods established in the auctions? (By the bids of the people who wanted to buy them.)

- Where did the people who had macaroni money get their bean money to trade in the auction that required bean money? (They got it from people with bean money who wanted macaroni money to trade in the auction that required macaroni money.)

- What determined the prices of goods in the country with macaroni money? (The quantity of money available relative to the goods available to be purchased. What individual purchasers were able and willing to pay was determined by their income in macaroni money, their preferences for the available goods, and the incomes and preferences of other bidders.)

- What determined the prices of goods in the country with bean money? (The quantity of money available relative to the goods available to be purchased. What individual purchasers were able and willing to pay was determined by their income in bean money, their preferences for the available goods, and the incomes and preferences of other bidders.)

- When money trading was allowed, what determined the exchange rate between macaroni money and bean money? (The purchasing power of each in its own country.)

ACTIVITY 1

16. Distribute Activity 1, *Money Markets*, and allow students sufficient time to read and answer the questions. Have the students work in small groups to share calculators and to allow more able students to help less able students.

17. Discuss the answers to the questions from the activity. (Answers: 1990 Total expenditures $47.97 . yen 6955.65 , Canadian dollars 56.12, pounds 26.86 .

1993 Total expenditures $47.97 . yen 5328.51 , Canadian dollars 61.88 , pounds 32.14.

The price of the goods in yen decreased. The price of the goods in Canadian dollars and British pounds increased. The purchasing power of the Japanese yen increased relative to the purchasing power of the U.S. dollar. The purchasing power of the Canadian dollar and the British pound decreased relative to the purchasing power of the U.S. dollar.)

18. Ask the students if they can explain why the exchange rates shown in the chart changed from 1990 to 1993. (The answer to this question is not obvious from the activity. Allow the students time to think about possible reasons, but be prepared to explain the following reasons to them. Compared to the dollar, the purchasing power of the yen went up while the purchasing power of the Canadian dollar and the pound went down. American exports became more attractive to Japanese consumers and Japanese imports less attractive to American consumers. American exports became less attractive to Canadian and British consumers, and Canadian and British imports were more attractive to American consumers.)

CLOSURE

Discuss the following questions:

- How did the available quantity of goods and services differ between the auctions and the money market activity? (The auctions involved fixed quantities of goods and money. In the real world, the United States, Japan, Canada and Great Britain could and probably did vary their output of goods and services, and the size of their money supplies changed as well.)

- Where did the dollars come from that were bought with yen, Canadian dollars, and pounds? (They came from people who had dollars and wanted yen, Canadian dollars, and pounds to buy goods in Japan, Canada, and the United Kingdom. American exports created a demand for dollars on the part of foreigners and generated a supply of foreign exchange for Americans, and American imports created a demand for foreign exchange on the part of Americans and generated a supply of dollars for foreigners.)

- What is the function of money in domestic markets? (It facilitates trade.)

- What is the function of foreign exchange markets? (They facilitate international trade.)

EVALUATION

- Put the information in the chart from Activity 1, *Money Markets*, on the chalkboard or on a transparency. Divide students into groups of three and tell them to have each group member select a different one of the foreign currencies listed on the table. Show students several items with large tags attached, displaying prices in American dollars. Tell them to compute the prices in each of their currencies using the 1993 scale.

- Ask the students to write a paragraph answering the following: What are foreign exchange and foreign exchange rates? Who demands and who supplies a particular foreign exchange, such as the peso? Why is a buyer in foreign exchange markets always a seller also?

EXTENSION ACTIVITIES

1. Ask the students to refer to the chart of exchange rates in Activity 1, *Money Markets*. If purchasing power of each of the currencies is the same worldwide, how would you determine the exchange rate between the yen and the Canadian dollar? What would be the yen price of a Canadian dollar in 1993? (You would divide the yen price for a dollar by the Canadian price for a dollar, 111.08 yen divided by 1.29 Canadian dollars. A Canadian dollar would cost 86.11 yen.)

2. Ask the students to refer to the chart of exchange rates in Activity 1, *Money Markets*. If in 1993 you bought an Irish wool sweater for 87.1 pounds, a Japanese made car for 1,625,655.80 yen, and a vacation in Canada that cost 3,225

Canadian dollars, how many American dollars would these purchases have cost you? (For the sweater, 87.1 pounds divided by .67 equals $130. For the car, 1,625,655.80 yen divided by 111.08 equals $14,635. For the vacation, 3,225 Canadian dollars divided by 1.29 equals $2,500. Total spending equals $17,265.)

ACTIVITY 1
MONEY MARKETS

Name _____

Trade between different countries is not very different from trade between regions of the same country. Maine ships potatoes to Florida, and Florida ships oranges to Maine, and the people in both states benefit. Countries trade for many of the same reasons as these states. For example, the United States sells computers, and Costa Rica sells bananas in world markets.

World trade, of course, is a lot more complex. Different countries use different kinds of money. They have different political systems. And they speak different languages. But the basic idea is the same.

The United States uses dollars for money. When people from other countries want to buy goods and services from American firms, they must pay in American dollars. When Americans want to buy foreign products, they must pay in foreign money. People and businesses get the foreign money they need by buying it in **foreign exchange markets**.

Foreign exchange markets are just like other markets. Instead of buying and selling goods and services, people buy and sell money. Those Americans who want to buy goods from France create a **demand** for French money called francs. Those people in France, who want to buy goods from the United States, exchange their francs for dollars and provide the **supply** of francs for Americans.

The following chart shows the average exchange rates between the American dollar, the Japanese yen, the Canadian dollar, and the British pound from 1990 through 1993.

Year	Yen Per Dollar	Canadian Dollar Per Dollar	Pound Per Dollar
1990	145.00	1.17	.56
1991	134.59	1.15	.57
1992	126.78	1.21	.57
1993	111.08	1.29	.67

Source: *Economic Report of the President, 1994,* Table B-110.

Pretend for the moment that the year is 1990. You are watching your favorite video, wearing a sweatshirt with your favorite logo on it, and eating a sandwich. You bought the video for $15.98, the sweatshirt for $30.00, and the sandwich for $1.99.

* What were your total expenditures? _____.

* How many yen would a Japanese tourist have paid for the same products? _____.

* How many Canadian dollars would a Canadian tourist have paid? _____.

* How many dollars would a British tourist have paid? _____.

ACTIVITY 1 (continued)

If these same products were exported to Japan, Canada, or Britain, you would have to add on transportation costs, importer's costs and profit, and taxes to obtain the market prices in yen, Canadian dollars, or pounds. If importers charge more than these totals, other importers will enter the market and drive down the prices.

Now pretend that it is 1993, and the prices in United States dollars have not changed.

• What are the new prices in Japanese yen? _____.

• What are the new prices in Canadian dollars? _____.

• What are the new prices in British pounds? _____.

• Describe what has happened to the prices of goods in each of the foreign currencies.

_____

_____

ACTIVITY 2
COUNTRY A GOODS

FOOTBALL CARD	BALLPOINT PEN	MOVIE POSTER
Player Name		_Name of Film_
FOOTBALL CARD	HOLIDAY PENCIL	MOVIE POSTER
Player Name	_Holiday Name_	_Name of Film_
HOCKEY CARD	HOLIDAY PENCIL	GREETING CARD
Player Name	_Holiday Name_	_Name of Occasion_
BASKETBALL CARD	RUBBER STAMP of Student's Name	COLORED PENCIL
Player Name		_Pencil Color_
BASEBALL CARD	RUBBER STAMP of Student's Name	COLORED MARKER
Player Name		_Marker Color_
BASEBALL CARD	RUBBER STAMP of Student's Name	COLORED MARKER
Player Name		_Marker Color_
ONE-HALF PINT CARTON OF MILK	COLLEGE T-SHIRT	MOVIE PASS
	Name of College	_Name of Film_
ONE-HALF PINT CARTON OF ORANGE JUICE	MUSIC TAPE	VIDEO RENTAL
	Name of Artist	_Name of Film_
ONE-HALF PINT CARTON OF MILK	COMPACT DISC	COMIC BOOK
	Name of Artist	_Name of Comic_
APPLE	BANANA	COMIC BOOK
		Name of Comic

ACTIVITY 2
COUNTRY B GOODS

BASKETBALL CARD _____ Player Name	**HOLIDAY PENCIL** _____ Holiday Name	**GREETING CARD** _____ Name of Occasion
BASKETBALL CARD _____ Player Name	**BALLPOINT PEN**	**GREETING CARD** _____ Name of Occasion
FOOTBALL CARD _____ Player Name	**BALLPOINT PEN**	**MOVIE POSTER** _____ Name of Film
FOOTBALL CARD _____ Player Name	**RULER**	**COLORED MARKER** _____ Marker Color
HOCKEY CARD _____ Player Name	**RULER**	**COLORED PENCIL** _____ Pencil Color
BASEBALL CARD _____ Player Name	**RULER**	**COLORED PENCIL** _____ Pencil Color
ONE-HALF PINT CARTON OF ORANGE JUICE	**COLLEGE CAP** _____ Name of College	**VIDEO RENTAL** _____ Name of Film
ONE-HALF PINT CARTON OF MILK	**MUSIC TAPE** _____ Name of Artist	**MOVIE PASS** _____ Name of Film
ONE-HALF PINT CARTON OF ORANGE JUICE	**COMPACT DISC** _____ Name of Artist	**STUFFED ANIMAL** _____ Name of Animal
BANANA	**APPLE**	**STUFFED ANIMAL** _____ Name of Animal

From _Geography: Focus on Economics,_ © National Council on Economic Education, New York, NY

LESSON SIX
LIMITING TRADE

INTRODUCTION

Despite the advantages of free trade, many nations impose limits on trade for a variety of reasons. The main types of trade restrictions are tariffs, quotas, embargoes, licensing requirements, standards, and subsidies.

Tariffs, taxes on imports, raise the price of imported goods, which increases the demand and price for the same goods produced by domestic suppliers. Revenues from tariffs are collected by the domestic government.

Quotas put a legal limit on the amount that can be imported, creating shortages which cause prices to rise. A quota benefits domestic producers in the same way a tariff does, but the additional money expended on foreign goods goes to the foreign producers, not the domestic government.

Embargoes prohibit trade with other nations. They bar a foreign nation's imports or ban exports to that nation or both.

Licenses may be required of importers of foreign goods so that imports can be restricted by limiting the number of licenses issued. Export licenses may be required in order to implement partial embargoes on trade with specific nations.

Standards are laws or regulations establishing health and safety standards for imported goods, frequently much stricter than those applied to domestically produced goods.

Subsidies are payments made by governments to their domestic producers to enable them to compete with foreign competitors. They are usually intended to be temporary, allowing domestic producers to acquire new technology or to survive a short-term problem, but they frequently linger on for many years. It is difficult to dislodge entrenched special interests. Taxpayers bear the costs of subsidy payments.

Trade restrictions limit world trade, diminish economic efficiency, reduce total production and employment, raise prices, and encourage retaliation. They benefit some domestic companies and their workers at the expense of foreign companies and workers, and domestic consumers. While subsidies benefit some domestic companies and workers in exporting industries, tariffs reduce exports. Tariffs shift resources and production from more effective to less effective producers.

Arguments used to support trade restrictions include the **infant industry** argument and the national security or **strategic industry** argument.

CONCEPTS

Tariffs
Quotas
Embargoes
Licensing Requirements
Standards (health and safety)
Subsidies
Infant Industry
Strategic Industry
Exports
Imports
Terms of Trade

OBJECTIVES

◆ Engage in a debate over the merits of a proposed tariff.

◆ Apply arguments in favor of and against tariffs to the debate situation.

◆ Evaluate the arguments presented in the debate.

◆ Analyze the costs and benefits of instituting a tariff.

LESSON DESCRIPTION

Students read a narrative describing various types of trade restrictions and their effects, engage in a circle debate about the imposition of a new tariff, evaluate the arguments in favor of and against the tariff, and apply the model described in the narrative to determine who will benefit and who will be hurt by the tariff.

TIME REQUIRED

One to two class periods.

MATERIALS

One or two blank transparencies or ditto masters
Pen to write on the transparencies
★One copy of Activity 1, *Trade Restrictions and Their Effects*, for each student.

PROCEDURE

1. Distribute Activity 1, *Trade Restrictions and Their Effects*. Explain to the students that they will be using this information in a debate activity. Allow students time to read the narrative. You may want to let them do the reading at the end of the period the day before you have the debate or assign the reading as homework.

2. Explain to the students that they are going to take part in an activity designed to help them understand trade restrictions and their effects.

3. Review the content in Activity 1, *Trade Restrictions and Their Effects*, with the class. If you have students who find the reading in the activity difficult, you may want to go over it with them, a paragraph at a time.

4. Choose one student to be a recorder. Provide him or her with a transparency and a pen suitable for writing on it, or with a ditto master. Tell the recorder to copy the written statements after they have been announced.

5. Divide the remaining students into two groups. Each group will argue one side of the question, "Should a tariff be imposed?" Group A will take the side of some small athletic shoe manufacturers. These companies are the major industries in the towns where they are located. Their workers are skilled and dedicated and are paid above average wages. Now these companies are facing competition from foreign companies that produce less expensive athletic shoes. The local companies are asking for government help in the form of a tariff on all imported shoes. Group B opposes the tariff on shoes. Both groups should refer to Activity 1, *Trade Restrictions and Their Effects*, for the pros and cons of imposing a tariff or other trade restrictions.

6. The discussion will take the form of a circle debate. Have each side sit in a circle. The members of each group should look at each other, not at the members of the other group. Have one student sit between the two circles and act as a recorder.

7. Group A, the group arguing in favor of a tariff, should begin. The group has 1 1/2 minutes to write a one-sentence statement of its position. Then one person from Group A should address the statement to Group B. The recorder should write the statement on a transparency or a ditto master.

8. Group B then has 1 1/2 minutes to decide on a counterstatement to Group A. Again, the recorder writes down the statement.

9. While Group B is deciding on its statement, members of Group A should be trying to guess what the statement will be. They also should be planning their own responses one or two turns ahead in the debate.

10. The debate continues, with each side offering reasons for its position, until one side convinces the other or until time runs out.

11. When the debate is finished, use the transparency or run off what was written by the recorder on the ditto master to help you discuss the debate and the issues.

CLOSURE

• Ask each student to write a paragraph that describes who will benefit and who will be hurt if the tariff on shoes is instituted. (Domestic owners and workers in the shoe industry will benefit. Local businesses in the towns where the shoe factories are located may also benefit. To the extent that foreign shoes are imported, the government imposing the tariff will obtain additional revenue. Foreign owners and workers in the shoe industry, and domestic consumers in the country imposing the tariff will be hurt. Because the purchase of imports decreases, foreigners will have less income to purchase exports from the country imposing the tariff. This will hurt

★ all students–basic course material
■ average and above average students
○ average and below average students

owners and work s in exporting industries.
Domestic produc on of shoes will increase,
prices of shoes w increase, and resources
will be diverted from more efficient industries
to the less efficient shoe industry.)

EVALUATION

• Ask students to think of an item that they
often use that may have come from another
country. Tell them to write a paragraph about
how different types of trade restrictions might
change or restrict their use of this product.

• Divide students into groups of about five students each. Let each group choose an imported good for their group to work with. Tell
students that each group member should take
the role of either (1) a foreign producer of the
product, (2) a domestic importer of the product, (3) a domestic consumer of the product,
4) a domestic producer of the same product, or
(5) a worker in a domestic factory producing
the same product. Have each member of the
group write or tell (recorded on audiotape)
how the passage of a trade restriction will
affect her or his life.

EXTENSION ACTIVITIES

1. Students can research why export taxes are
prohibited in the United States Constitution,
determine who would benefit from such taxes, and
what their impact would have been on the United
States economy in 1790.

2. Students can research and report on the
General Agreement on Tariffs and Trade, concen-
trating on the eighth round of negotiations, which
began in Uruguay in 1986. They should discuss
what progress has been made toward eliminating
trade barriers and domestic subsidies in agriculture, removing barriers to trade in services, end-
ing restrictions on foreign economic investments,
and establishing and enforcing patent, copyright,
and trademark rights, so-called intellectual property rights, on an international basis.

3. Students can research and report on recent
actions of the United States that restricted international trade: the voluntary agreement reached
with Japan in 1981 to limit the number of

Japanese automobiles imported to the United
States (the agreement expired in 1985 but was
continued informally), the 1982 import quotas
imposed on sugar, the 1982 voluntary agreement
with the Common Market nations, which imposed
a quota on their steel exports to the United States,
and the 1990 law, passed by both houses of
Congress but vetoed by President Reagan, that
protected the U.S. textile industry. (It would be
very instructive to read the debate to override the
president's veto in the Congressional Record.)

ACTIVITY 1
TRADE RESTRICTIONS AND THEIR EFFECTS

When nations specialize and trade, total world output is increased. Companies produce for foreign markets as well as *domestic markets* (markets in the home country). **Exports** are the goods and services sold in foreign markets. **Imports** are goods or services bought from foreign producers.

In spite of the benefits of international trade, many nations put limits on trade for various reasons. The main types of trade restrictions are tariffs, quotas, embargoes, licensing requirements, standards, and subsidies.

A **tariff** is a tax put on goods imported from abroad. The effect of a tariff is to raise the price of the imported product. It helps domestic producers of similar products to sell them at higher prices. The money received from the tariff is collected by the domestic government.

A **quota** is a limit on the amount of goods that can be imported. Putting a quota on a good creates a shortage, which causes the price of the good to rise and allows domestic producers to raise their prices and to expand their production. A quota on shoes, for example, might limit foreign-made shoes to 10,000,000 pairs a year. If Americans buy 200,000,000 pairs of shoes each year, this would leave most of the market to American producers.

An **embargo** stops exports or imports of a product or group of products to or from another country. Sometimes all trade with a country is stopped, usually for political reasons.

Some countries require import or export **licenses**. When domestic importers of foreign goods are required to get licenses, imports can be restricted by not issuing many licenses. Export licenses have been used to restrict trade with certain countries or to keep domestic prices on agricultural products from rising.

Standards are laws or regulations that nations use to restrict imports. Sometimes nations establish health and safety standards for imported goods that are higher than those for goods produced domestically. These have become a major form of trade restriction and are used in different amounts by many countries.

Subsidies can be thought of as tariffs in reverse. Instead of taxing the foreign import, the government gives grants of money to *domestic* producers to encourage exports. Those who receive such subsidies can use them to pay production costs and can charge less for their goods than foreign producers. A tariff is paid for by the buyers of the foreign goods and the buyers of domestic goods who pay higher prices. But subsidies are paid for by taxpayers who may or may not use the good.

What are the effects of these trade restrictions?
- They all limit world trade, which means a reduction in the total number of goods and services produced.

- They shift production from more effective exporting producers to less effective domestic producers.

- When production is lowered, there are fewer workers earning income. Trade restrictions also raise prices, which is usually their main purpose.

- Trade limits in one country, moreover, usually lead to limits being imposed in other countries. If the United States places a high tariff on cars made in Japan, for example, Japan may then put tariffs on American goods sold in Japan.

In spite of these disadvantages, countries are tempted to use trade restrictions to protect their own industries. Countries that are just getting started use tariffs, quotas, and subsidies to protect their industries until they can compete without government help. The difficulty with this **infant industry** argument in support of trade restrictions is that it is not always possible to predict which

ACTIVITY 1 (continued)

industries will succeed. Protection frequently lasts long after the industry has matured.

Governments are eager to protect what are called **strategic industries**. These have included industries, such as steel, cars, chemicals, and munitions, that are important during a war. Today, they are more often the high tech, high wage industries like commercial aircraft production. One way of insuring that they remain strong is to protect them from foreign competition. Agriculture is another area that many govern-ments try to protect. Tariffs and subsidies help make sure that domestic farmers can earn enough profits to continue farming.

The decision to use trade restrictions like tariffs is an important one. Tariffs help some domestic industries, but they mean higher prices for buy-ers. They help the owners and workers in the pro-tected industries. They hurt the people who have to pay higher prices for the goods those industries make. Reducing imports reduces the income of foreigners. They will reduce their foreign pur-chases, hurting exporting industries and workers in the nation that put the tariff on the imports. Without much competition, companies may also use less efficient production methods. This can lead to poorer quality as well.

It is in the best interest of the world economy for each nation to specialize in the goods it makes best and to trade freely with all other nations. However, this practice does not always benefit every nation. For example, exporters who control a large part of the world's supply of a product can use trade restrictions to change the **terms of trade**, reducing the amount of their goods and services they must give up to obtain imports. This was done by the Organization of Petroleum Exporting Countries (OPEC) when they restricted their output of oil in the 1970s. By driving up the price of oil they were able to get more imports for less oil.

Most arguments for trade restriction benefit pro-tected industries and their workers. They also create much greater losses for a nation's economy. In the long run, a nation must import to export.

LESSON SEVEN
PLACES AND PRODUCTION

INTRODUCTION

Gross Domestic Product (GDP), a basic measure of economic output, is the total market value of all final goods and services produced in an economy in a given year. Although GDP does not account for differences in the types of goods produced, nor for differences in the distribution of income, **GDP per capita** (GDP divided by population) is often used to compare the economies of countries and the well-being of their citizens.

Geographers apply a spatial perspective to economic and social data using **choropleth maps**. A choropleth map shows differences between areas. Distinct categories of *qualities* can be represented by different colors or shading patterns. Four different colors could represent deserts, mountains, forests, and grasslands, for example. Choropleth maps can be used to display differences in *quantities* as well. The range of population density can be divided into five to ten categories. Each category is then assigned a color or shading pattern, and each area on the map is colored based on its category of population density. Regional concentrations of population and areas of sparse population could be easily identified with such a map.

Choropleth maps that display economic data aid in the analysis of that data. This lesson uses choropleth maps of GDP per capita. This technique will be used in subsequent lessons with other measures of well-being.

CONCEPTS

Gross Domestic Product (GDP)
Choropleth Map
Measure of Value
Double Counting
Final Goods and Services
Flow of Product Approach
Earnings and Cost Approach
Consumer Spending

Investment Spending
Government Spending
Exports
Imports
Gross Domestic Product Per Capita

OBJECTIVES

◆   Calculate GDP and GDP per capita.

◆   Acquire information from a choropleth map.

◆   Construct a choropleth map.

◆   Recognize the uses and limitations of GDP as a measure of economic well-being.

LESSON DESCRIPTION

Students calculate United States GDP and GDP per capita, use a choropleth map to acquire information, and create choropleth maps of GDP per capita in South America. They identify regions with high and low GDP per capita and suggest reasons why the well-being of people may be overestimated in countries with high GDP per capita and underestimated in countries with low GDP per capita.

TIME REQUIRED

One to two class periods.

MATERIALS

One copy for each student of
○ Activity 1, *Gross Domestic Product,* and
★ Activity 2, *Constructing a Choropleth Map.*
One copy of Activity 3, *Map of South America,* for each student.
One transparency of Visual 1, *Choropleth World Map of GDP Per Capita.*
Classroom set of atlases with maps of South America and the World (Students should be able to share atlases.)
An assortment of colored pencils, markers, or crayons.

PROCEDURE

1. Tell the class that this lesson is about Gross Domestic Product (GDP), a measure of economic production, which is used by economists and geographers as a measure of well-being. GDP is the total market value of all the final goods and ser-

★ all students–basic course material
■ average and above average students
○ average and below average students

vices produced in an economy in a given year.

2. Distribute Activity 1, *Gross Domestic Product*, and ask the students to read the explanation of GDP and to answer question 1. If the reading is too difficult for your students, go through it with the students, paragraph by paragraph. (United States GDP for 1993 was $6,374.0 billion.)

3. Review the information from Activity 1, *Gross Domestic Product*, to be certain students understand:
   • Definitions of GDP.
   • Calculating GDP using the total spending method.
   • Limitations of GDP as an indicator of economic well-being.

4. Explain GDP per capita and have students answer question 2. (United States GDP per capita for 1993 was $24,683.)

5. Display the transparency of Visual 1, *Choropleth World Map of GDP Per Capita*. Explain that this is a choropleth map that will be used to analyze regional variations in GDP per capita. Tell the students that the range of GDP per capita is $80 to $32,790. That range has been divided into 9 categories which are shown in the *legend* or *key*. Each category has a shading pattern associated with it, and each country is shaded according to its category.

Ask the students to complete the following statements:

   • The GDP per capita of Canada is between $ _____ and $ _____.

   • Four countries with GDP per capita between $15,000 and $19,999 are _____, _____, _____, and _____.

   • The nations of South America have GDP per capita between $ _____ and $_____.

(GDP per capita of Canada is between $20,000 and $24,999. Four countries with GDP per capita

between $15,000 and $19,999 are <u>Great Britain</u>, <u>France</u>, <u>Italy</u>, and <u>Australia</u>. The nations of South America have GDP per capita between <u>$300</u> and <u>$4,999</u>.)

6. Distribute Activity 2, *Constructing a Choropleth Map*, and ask the students to read the first three paragraphs, which describe choropleth maps. Go over the directions for creating a choropleth map with the students and answer any questions that they have about the process.

7. Distribute Activity 3, *Map of South America*. Have each student construct a choropleth map of GDP per capita in South America. Allow students to work in pairs if they choose. (Tell the students who are having trouble getting started that the range of values from 370 to 3050 is 2680, close to 2700, and that nine mapping categories of 300 units will work well. The sample that follows is only a suggested answer. There are many other possibilities.)

CLOSURE

Display the transparency of Visual 1, *Choropleth World Map of GDP Per Capita*. Some countries may be blank because they do not report data or may report it in a form not easily converted to GDP in dollars. Ask the following questions:

• Where are the countries with high GDP per capita (top four categories) located? (In general, the northern hemisphere. Students should mention continents like North America, and regions like Northern and Western Europe or Western Asia, but they may tell you about individual countries such as Japan, Italy, and Australia.)

• Where are the countries with low GDP per capita (bottom three categories) located? (South America, Central America, Africa, Asia, Eastern Europe, and the Caribbean.)

• Why might the well-being of people in low GDP per capita countries be underestimated? (GDP per capita does not include goods and services not sold in the marketplace. When people grow their own food, build their own shelter, and make their own clothes, those goods and services are not included in their country's GDP.)

- How can a nation increase its GDP? (Point out that for an economy to become more productive it must produce fewer goods for domestic consumption and more capital goods. It is investment that increases the productivity of workers, including investment in the workers themselves, increasing the quality of their human capital. Such investments have significant opportunity costs and economic risks.)

EVALUATION

- Ask the students to create choropleth maps of the United States using the data on *Population Per Square Mile* or *Gross State Product Per Capita* from Activity 2, *State Population and*

Economic Statistics, found in Lesson 10, *Which State Is the Largest?*

- Ask the students to create posters illustrating the components of Gross Domestic Product, using the flow of product approach.

EXTENSION ACTIVITY

1. Ask students to select a country with a high GDP per capita and a country with a low GDP per capita and, using geography textbooks, periodical articles, atlases, encyclopedias, and other sources, to research those countries in order to write reports describing similarities and differences between their countries and the factors that account for the differences in GDP per capita.

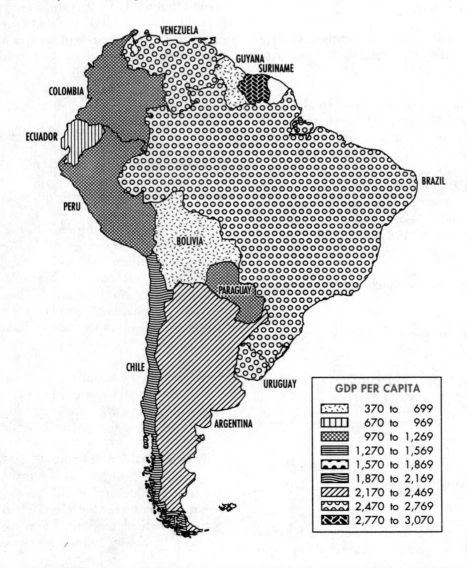

GDP PER CAPITA	
	370 to 699
	670 to 969
	970 to 1,269
	1,270 to 1,569
	1,570 to 1,869
	1,870 to 2,169
	2,170 to 2,469
	2,470 to 2,769
	2,770 to 3,070

ACTIVITY 1
GROSS DOMESTIC PRODUCT

Name _____

Gross Domestic Product (GDP) is a statistic that shows the value of goods and services produced in a country in a particular year. All of the goods and services that are sold each year have to be counted. Every new car and truck, every egg laid by every hen, every CD, every doughnut, burger, and taco has to be included. Services must be counted, too. Barbers, nurses, lawyers, computer programmers, and basketball players sell their services and these services are part of GDP. Suppose all of these things and many more besides were stacked up in one big pile. It would still be hard to know the value of all the goods and services produced by the economy, yet this is what the Gross Domestic Product (GDP) tries to measure.

How is it done? First, instead of counting the actual goods made and sold and all of the services performed, economists add up what these things sold for in dollars and cents. In other words, they are using money as a **measure of value**. So, if people buy 2,000,000 bushels of apples at $1 per bushel, and 2,000,000 books at $1 per book, these purchases add $4,000,000 to the Gross Domestic Product.

Second, not everything made and sold during the year can be counted. For example, the paper in your math book was once part of a giant roll of paper in a paper mill. Some people worked hard to make that roll of paper, and others worked hard to make your book. Both the roll of paper and the book are goods. But if the money paid for both the roll of paper and the book were counted, the value of the paper would be counted twice. So to avoid this problem of **double counting**, economists only count a product in its final form. They count the paper, for example, in its final product form as a book, a newspaper, a magazine, or a shopping bag. They refer to these as **final goods and services**.

There are two different ways of counting the

value of goods and services, but they both give the same answer. The first way, the **flow of product approach**, is by counting all the money spent by the buyers of goods and services. The second way, **the earnings and cost approach**, is by counting all the money received by those who produce the goods and services. Each of these ways looks at different sides of the same economic activities. If a person makes a chair and sells it for $50, both seller and buyer have helped increase the Gross Domestic Product by $50. In figuring out what the Gross Domestic Product is, an economist might count the $50 the buyer spent for the chair, using the flow of product approach. But he might count the $20 that went to the lumber yard owner, the $5 that went to the paint store owner, the $5 for wear and tear on tools used in making the chair, and the $20 for the cost of labor, instead. These are the payments that were made for the resources that were used to produce the chair, and this example of the earnings and cost approach also adds up to $50.

If the Gross Domestic Product is computed using the flow of product approach and counting what people spend, four different kinds of spending must be taken into account. These are:
* consumption: spending by ordinary consumers,
* investment: spending by businesses on new equipment,
* spending by all levels of Government, and
* spending by foreigners who buy American goods (our exports) minus spending by Americans on foreign goods (our imports).

Of course, no way of adding up the Gross Domestic Product can be entirely accurate. But the two ways discussed here give a rough estimate of the total value of what the economy produces in a given year. Better still, measuring the Gross Domestic Product each year can show if the economy is growing or shrinking, healthy or sick. It is a standard by which the economy as a whole can

ACTIVITY 1 (continued)

be judged. It can be used to compare one economy with another. It can also be used to compare an economy with itself over time.

Symbolically, GDP is represented by the equation:

$$GDP = C + I + G + (X - M)$$

The letters in this equation represent the four kinds of spending mentioned above. C is consumer spending, I is business investment spending, G is government spending, X is the spending by foreigners on the nation's exports, and M is the spending on imported goods from foreign nations. The figures below show the levels of spending in *billions of dollars* for the United States economy in 1993.

Consumer Spending	4,390.6
Investment Spending	892.0
Government Spending	1,157.1
Exports	660.1
Imports	725.8

Source: *Economic Report of the President, 1994*

1. Using the GDP equation above, calculate the United States GDP for 1993. _____

Gross Domestic Product per capita is the amount of GDP that would be available for each person to use if a country's production of goods and services were divided equally among its people. *Capita* is the Latin word for *head*, so GDP per capita means GDP per person. GDP per capita is one way to determine how well-off the average person is in a country.

2. Calculate the United States GDP per capita by dividing the GDP obtained above by the 1993 population. The population of the United States in 1993 was 258,233,000. _____

GDP does not show the types or quality of goods and services that a country produces. GDP per capita shows an average standard of living, and it does not show how many people in a country are richer or poorer than the average. People in countries that have similar levels of GDP per capita may share goods and services in very different ways.

GDP has other limitations as a measure of economic well-being. It does not include items such as goods and services not sold in the marketplace such as cooking, repairing one's own car, mowing the lawn, painting the garage, and other unpaid work done at home. The value of leisure time, and illegal goods and services are not added to GDP, and negative goods, such as pollution, that detract from well-being are not subtracted.

Despite its limitations, GDP is a powerful measure of economic welfare. It can be used in combination with other measures to assess the welfare of people throughout the world.

From *Geography: Focus on Economics,* © National Council on Economic Education, New York, NY

VISUAL 1
CHOROPLETH MAP OF GDP PER CAPITA

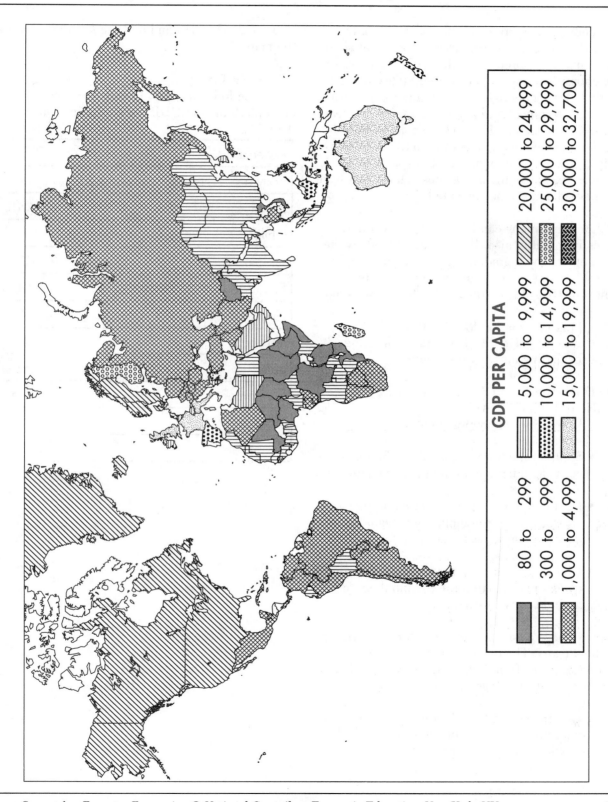

ACTIVITY 2
CONSTRUCTING A CHOROPLETH MAP

A choropleth map uses colors or shading to show differences between areas. Areas that share a quality are colored or shaded alike. A very simple choropleth map of the United States could be made by using a single color or shading pattern to show those states that have a state sales tax, leaving the other states blank. Three colors would be needed to show those states that have state sales taxes, state income taxes, and both sales and income taxes, leaving blank those states that have neither sales taxes nor income taxes.

Choropleth maps can be used to show differences in quantity also. If you wanted to show the percent of people graduating from high school on a world map, you could use ten colors to represent 0 to 10%, 11 to 20%, 21 to 30%, and so on.

Mapping information locates it for you. You know *where* it exists. And you have a starting point for finding out why it is there.

DIRECTIONS FOR CREATING A CHOROPLETH MAP

1. Determine the mapping categories.

- Subtract the lowest value from the highest value to calculate the range of the numbers.

- Decide upon the number of mapping categories. Five to ten mapping categories are adequate for most maps.

- Divide the range by the number of mapping categories to determine the numbers to include in each category.

2. Choose a color code or shading pattern for each category. The colors or patterns assigned should increase from light to dark to represent the lowest to highest category.

3. Locate and label each country on an outline map, determine its mapping category, and color or shade the country appropriately.

4. Title the map and add the *key* or *legend* to the map.

ASSIGNMENT

Use the following data to construct your own choropleth map of GDP per capita in South America.

Argentina	2,365
Bolivia	620
Brazil	2,680
Chile	1,940
Colombia	1,240
Ecuador	960
Guyana	370
Paraguay	1,110
Peru	1,160
Suriname	3,050
Uruguay	2,560
Venezuela	2,560

*In 1990 U.S. dollars.
Source: *Population Data Sheet,* Population Reference Bureau, Inc., April 1992.

From *Geography: Focus on Economics,* © National Council on Economic Education, New York, NY

ACTIVITY 3
MAP OF SOUTH AMERICA

LESSON EIGHT GDP AND LIFE EXPECTANCY

INTRODUCTION

Choropleth maps display data by political boundary. Areas that share a quality are given the same color or shading. Maps in history books that show the Union states as blue and the Confederate states as gray are choropleth maps. Choropleth maps are also used to display quantitative data. The number of doctors per square mile can be obtained for each state. Then, based on the range of values, the number of categories is chosen. Each category is given a color or a shading pattern, and each state is colored according to the category it fits. Choropleth maps are frequently used to explore relationships among economic and social variables. The maps provide a spatial dimension that other forms of data presentation lack.

Gross Domestic Product per capita is a measure of the total value of all the final goods and services produced in a nation during a year divided by the population of the nation. It shows what each person's share of the nation's production would be if it were divided equally.

GDP per capita is positively related to **life expectancy**. People who live in countries with high levels of GDP tend to live longer. They generally have a lower percent of their population under age 15 and a higher percentage over age 65 than countries with low levels of GDP. Countries with low levels of GDP per capita earn high percentages of their GDP from agriculture, have shorter life expectancies, and high rates of **infant mortality** (death).

With few exceptions, you will find the countries with high levels of GDP per capita in the northern hemisphere. Seven of the highest ten GDP per capita countries are in Europe and two are in North America. Fourteen of the lowest twenty GDP per capita countries are in Africa and six are in Asia. This should lead to a recognition of the importance of physical geography for understanding the problems of regions with low GDP per capita.

Living standards throughout the world are directly related to labor productivity. A nation's potential GDP depends on the quantity and quality of natural resources available, the size and skills of the labor force, and the size and quality of its capital stock. Public health measures, free prenatal clinics, and other programs to lower the infant death rate in low GDP per capita countries will lead to an increase in the percent of the population under 15. But, unless **investment** in capital goods and in **human capital** can increase labor productivity in these countries, GDP per capita will remain stagnant or even decrease.

CONCEPTS

Choropleth Maps
Gross Domestic Product Per Capita
Life Expectancy
Infant Mortality
Investment
Human Capital
Positive Relationship
Negative Relationship

OBJECTIVES

◆ Construct choropleth maps illustrating the spatial dimensions of economic and social variables.

◆ Analyze relationships among variables using choropleth maps.

◆ Describe characteristics of countries with high and low GDP per capita.

◆ Locate regions of high and low GDP per capita.

◆ Hypothesize about the effects of measures designed to reduce infant mortality.

◆ Research the relationships among economics, environment, people, and health in Africa.

LESSON DESCRIPTION

Students construct choropleth maps based on a

number of economic and social variables, then analyze the relationships among the variables. They describe the characteristics of countries with high and low GDP per capita, identify regions of high and low GDP per capita, and generate hypotheses about possible consequences of efforts to improve the health of people in Africa.

TIME REQUIRED
Two class periods.

MATERIALS
★One copy for each student of Activity 1, *Comparing Choropleth Maps.*
Two copies for each student of Activity 2, *World Map.*
Visual 1, *Comparing Choropleth Maps.*
Atlases for students to share when making their maps.

PROCEDURE
1. Using the information in the *Introduction*, explain to the class what choropleth maps are. Tell the students that choropleth maps can be used to examine the ways that regions are similar and different. Explain that in this lesson they will construct choropleth maps to see how GDP per capita and other characteristics are related.

2. Distribute Activity 1, *Comparing Choropleth Maps,* and two copies of Activity 2, *World Map,* to each student. Tell the students to read Activity 1 and follow the directions for making the maps. Have the students work in pairs, letting one person construct a choropleth map based on GDP per capita while the other person constructs a choropleth map based on the percent of GDP that comes from agriculture.

3. When the students have completed their maps, ask them the following:

- Do the two variables, GDP per capita and percent of GDP that comes from agriculture, seem to be related? If so, how? Explain that there is a **negative relationship**. (Countries with high values for one variable have low values for the other variable.) High values for both variables or low values for both variables would be a **positive relationship**.

4. Ask each pair of students to select two additional variables to map. Be sure that at least one student in the class selects each of the remaining variables.

5. When the students have completed their maps, ask them the following:

- Do the two variables your team has mapped seem to be related? If so, is the relationship a positive relationship or a negative relationship? (Record the answers on the transparency of Visual 1, *Comparing Choropleth Maps.* The chart below shows the relationships between each variable and all the other variables.)

Answers for Visual 1

% Agriculture	Life Exp. Male	Life Exp. Female	% Pop. Under 15	% Pop. Over 65	Infant Deaths	
Negative	Positive	Positive	Negative	Positive	Negative	GDP Per Capita
	Negative	Negative	Positive	Negative	Positive	% Agriculture
		Positive	Negative	Positive	Negative	Life Exp. Male
			Negative	Positive	Negative	Life Exp. Female
				Negative	Positive	% Pop. Under 15
					Negative	% Pop. Over 65

6. Tell the students that this sample of countries contains 15 of the top 20 and 15 of the bottom 20 countries ranked by GDP per capita. For purpose of this activity any value that is above the middle, or *median value*, of any measure is considered high and any value that is below the median value is considered low. The median values are:

Percent of GDP from Agriculture	16.1
Life Expectancy Male	61.5
Life Expectancy Female	67.0
Percent of Population Under Age 15	37.0
Percent of Population Over Age 65	4.0
Infant Deaths Per 1000 Live Births	60.5

★ all students–basic course material
■ average and above average students
○ average and below average students

7. Ask each team to write a statement describing the characteristics of countries with high GDP per capita and a statement describing the characteristics of countries with low GDP per capita. (*Sample:* Countries with high GDP per capita have a low percent of their GDP from agriculture, have high life expectancies for both males and females, have a low percentage of their population under age 15 and a high percentage of their population over age 65, and have a low infant death rate.)

8. Remind the students that generalizing about countries can obscure interesting variations among them. For example, the United Arab Emirates has slightly lower life expectancies, a higher percentage of people under age 15, a much lower percentage of people over 65, and a higher infant death rate than the other high GDP per capita countries. Discuss possible reasons for these differences. (The United Arab Emirates is a relatively recent addition to the list of high GDP per capita countries based on its extensive oil resources. Improved public health programs and medical care have increased life expectancy and decreased the infant death rate, but more time is needed to bring these variables into line with those of the other high GDP per capita countries. Cultural factors and a very unequal distribution of wealth are additional factors that may be at work. They may also explain the percentage of the population under age 15.)

CLOSURE

Ask the following questions:

• Where are the countries with low GDP per capita located? (Seven in East Africa, four in Southern Asia, three in Western Africa, and one in Middle Africa.)

• Where are the countries with high GDP per capita located? (Five in Northern Europe, four in Western Europe, two in North America, one in Southern Europe, one in Western Asia, one in East Asia, and one in Oceania.)

• If high GDP per capita is an indication of economic well-being, what should be the long-term economic goal of low GDP per capita countries? (A country's potential GDP depends on the quantity and quality of natural resources available, the size and skills of the labor force, and the size and quality of its stock of capital goods. To increase GDP per capita an economy must become more productive. It can produce fewer goods for domestic consumption and more capital goods or it may sell goods to other countries and use the money to buy capital goods. It is investment that increases the productivity of workers, including investment in the workers themselves, increasing the quality of their human capital through education or training. Such investments have significant opportunity costs and economic risks. While one of the characteristics of many high GDP per capita countries is a low percentage of GDP from agriculture, countries facing famine may have to invest more rather than less in agriculture, at least until they establish a comparative advantage in the production of other goods and services.)

• What would be the effect of introducing public health measures, free prenatal clinics, and other programs to lower the infant death rate in Africa and Southern Asia? (The immediate effect would be an increase in the percent of the population under 15, and an increase in life expectancy at birth for males and females. Over time there may be an increase in the percent of the population over age 65, depending on the course of economic development. But a growing population without economic development would put additional strain on barely adequate food supplies. Famine and starvation, which already appear regularly, would become even more serious.)

EVALUATION

• Ask the students to choose a country from Table 1 of Activity 1, *Comparing Choropleth Maps*, and look over the statistics presented for that country. Then have them write a paragraph about a young child in this country, describing what life is probably like now, and what the outlook for the future might be.

EXTENSION ACTIVITIES

1. Africa's physical geography contributes to its problems of famine, inadequate and imbal-

anced diets, low life expectancies, and high infant mortality. It provides ideal breeding conditions for the mosquitoes, fleas, flies, and snails that carry debilitating diseases that kill millions and weaken millions more. Contaminated water supplies ensure that many Africans will be ill for their entire lives. Ask students to research the impact of endemic diseases like malaria, African sleeping sickness, yellow fever, and other diseases on people and livestock.

Ask the students to investigate why African nations haven't been able to deal with these health problems and whether these problems are tied to a low level of economic development as are the problems of infant mortality, short life expectancy, and low GDP per capita. Tell the students to look for any reasons to be optimistic about these problems. Have the students make oral reports to the class based upon their research.

2. Ask the students to turn to Table 1 of Activity 1. Draw their attention to the columns labeled *Life Expectancy Male* and *Life Expectancy Female*. Point out that for almost every country females have a longer life expectancy than males. Then ask the students to divide the countries into two groups, those countries with GDP per capita above $270 and those countries with GDP per capita of $270 or less. They should then calculate the average difference in life expectancy between men and women in the high GDP per capita group of countries. Women have a life expectancy 6.4 years longer than men. Repeating the process for the low GDP per capita group of countries will show that women have a life expectancy 2.27 years longer than men. Let each student pick one of the thirty countries to research and write a paragraph explaining the differences in life expectancy between women and men in their country. When the research is completed, conduct a class discussion to share findings.

ACTIVITY 1
COMPARING CHOROPLETH MAPS

A choropleth map displays data by political boundary. It uses colors or shading to show differences between areas. Areas that share a quality or have a similar value are colored the same. For example, choropleth maps can be used to show variation in average income. Countries with high average incomes are colored or shaded alike. Countries with low average incomes have their color, also. And countries with medium average have a third color. For most measures, five to ten categories are enough. When you have choropleth maps for several different statistics, you can compare the ways that countries are alike and different. You can see how regions of the world are alike and different also.

You are going to create choropleth maps in this activity. You will work with a partner on this. Each of you will have two blank world maps. Using the data on Table 1, one member of your team will construct a choropleth map based on GDP per capita while the other member of the team constructs a choropleth map based on the percent of GDP that comes from agriculture.

When you have completed your maps, you will be asked to select two additional variables from Table 1 to map.

DIRECTIONS FOR CREATING A CHORO-PLETH MAP

1. Determine the mapping categories.

    • Subtract the lowest value from the highest value to calculate the range of the numbers.

    • Decide upon the number of mapping categories. Five to ten mapping categories are adequate for most maps.

    • Divide the range by the number of mapping categories to determine the numbers to include in each category.

2. Choose a color code or shading pattern for each category. The colors or patterns assigned should increase from light to dark to represent the lowest to highest category.

3. Locate and label each country on an outline map, determine its mapping category, and color or shade the country appropriately.

4. Title the map and add the key or legend to the map.

From *Geography: Focus on Economics,* © National Council on Economic Education, New York, NY

ACTIVITY 1 (continued)

TABLE 1

Country	GDP Per Capita	% Of GDP From Agriculture	Life Expectancy At Birth		% Of Population		Infant Deaths Per 1000 Live Births
			Male	Female	Under Age 15	Over Age 65	
AFGHANISTAN	175	59.7	41	42	46	4	172.0
AUSTRALIA	17080	4.0	73	80	22	11	8.0
AUSTRIA	19240	3.2	73	79	17	15	7.4
BANGLADESH	200	42.7	54	53	44	3	120.0
BHUTAN	190	44.2	46	49	39	4	142.0
BURUNDI	210	56.5	50	54	46	3	111.0
CANADA	20450	3.2	73	80	22	11	8.0
CHAD	190	41.4	45	47	43	4	127.0
DENMARK	22090	4.6	72	78	17	16	7.5
ETHIOPIA	120	41.7	46	48	46	3	139.0
FINLAND	26070	6.2	71	79	19	13	5.8
FRANCE	19480	3.6	73	81	20	14	7.3
ITALY	16850	3.6	73	80	17	14	8.6
JAPAN	25430	2.4	76	82	18	13	4.6
LUXEMBOURG	28770	2.1	71	78	17	13	7.4
MALAGASY REPUBLIC	230	43.5	53	56	47	3	115.0
MALAWI	200	37.9	48	50	48	3	137.0
MALI REPUBLIC	270	39.6	43	46	47	4	113.0
NEPAL	170	58.7	50	50	42	3	112.0
NETHERLANDS	17330	4.7	74	80	18	13	6.8
NIGERIA	270	26.0	48	49	45	2	114.0
NORWAY	23120	3.0	73	80	19	16	6.9
SIERRA LEONE	240	39.0	41	44	44	3	147.0
SOMALI REPUBLIC	150	64.9	44	48	46	3	127.0
SWEDEN	23680	3.1	75	80	18	18	6.0
TANZANIA	120	56.1	49	54	48	3	105.0
UGANDA	220	66.9	50	52	49	2	96.0
UNITED ARAB EMIRATES	19860	1.7	69	73	35	1	25.0
UNITED KINGDOM	16070	1.4	73	79	19	16	7.9
UNITED STATES	21700	1.9	72	79	22	13	9.0

Source: *Population Data Sheet, Population Reference Bureau, April, 1992.*

ACTIVITY 2
WORLD MAP

Name _____

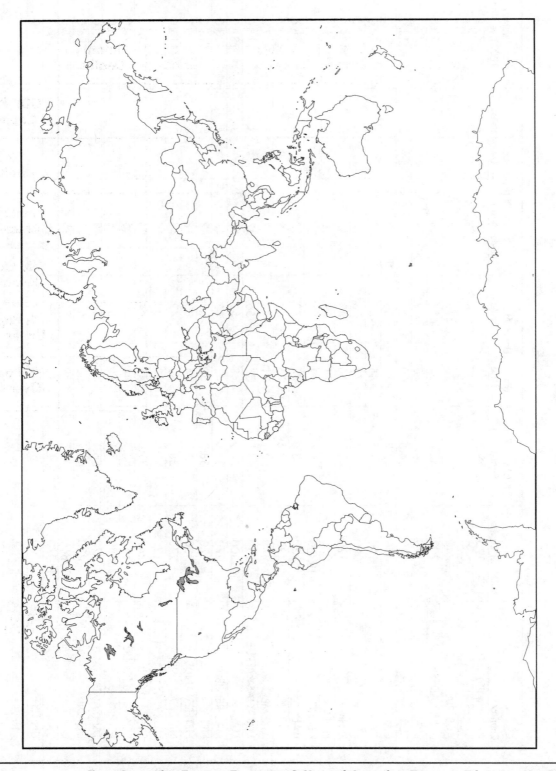

VISUAL 1
COMPARING CHOROPLETH MAPS

% Agriculture	Life Exp. Male	Life Exp. Female	% Pop. Under 15	% Pop. Over 65	Infant Deaths	
						GDP Per Capita
						% Agriculture
						Life Exp. Male
						Life Exp. Female
						% Pop. Under 15
						% Pop. Over 65

LESSON NINE
POPULATION PYRAMIDS

INTRODUCTION

Demography is the science dealing with sta-tistics of human population, including size, distri-bution, diseases, births and deaths. Demographers use **population pyramids** to show the distribu-tion of population by age and sex. These useful bar graphs can be compiled for neighborhoods, cities, states, and countries. Historians use popu-lation pyramids to show the effects of past events on birth and death rates and gender. Geographers use population pyramids to describe the charac-teristics, distribution, and migration of human populations on the earth's surface. Economists use population pyramids to determine what prod-ucts and social services might be in great demand for certain municipalities or countries, based on the ages and gender of their populations.

Students can use population pyramids to describe the structure of different populations and to analyze the effects of natural and human inter-actions on populations. Given the population pyramid of a region, they can generate hypotheses about major societal changes that might take place in that location in 10, 20, and 50 years. For example, a municipality or country with a large percentage of population under five years of age may want to plan for elementary school expansion in the very near future while a municipality or country with a large percentage of the population over 65 years of age will experience the increased health care demands of an elderly population.

Population pyramids are useful tools for organiz-ing data and are relatively easy to construct. In this lesson students create population pyramids from Census data, make hypotheses about communities from their population pyramids, and use population pyramids to analyze their own community.

CONCEPTS

Demography
Population Pyramid
Census
Median Age
Cohorts

OBJECTIVES

◆ Use population pyramids to describe the demographic structure of a population.

◆ Analyze the population characteristics of places to explain population patterns.

◆ Make predictions based on analysis of specific age cohorts.

◆ Understand the implications of their predictions for resource use, demand for goods and services, business opportunities, and government action.

LESSON DESCRIPTION

Students are introduced to demographic data and population pyramids using the 1990 Census of the United States. They are then organized into small groups, and each group is given population data for a community, asked to construct a popu-lation pyramid and to write a paragraph describ-ing its pyramid. The class discusses these pyramids and paragraphs and hypothesizes expla-nations for the demographic profiles of the com-munities. They discuss the implications of the observed demographic profiles for businesses and governmental agencies. Finally they apply the techniques learned to study their own community.

TIME REQUIRED

Two or three class periods.

MATERIALS

One copy for each student of
○ Activity 1, *United States Population.*
Calculators (optional, but helpful).
★ One copy of Activity 2A, 2B, 2C, or 2D for each pair or group of students.
One piece of graph paper for each pair or group of students.
Transparencies of Visual 1, *United States Population*; Visual 2, *United States Population Pyramid*; Visual 3 , *Anytown Population Pyramid*; Visual 4, *Suburbia Population Pyramid*; Visual 5, *Older City Population*

★ all students–basic course material
■ average and above average students
○ average and below average students

Pyramid; and Visual 6, *College Town Population Pyramid.*

PROCEDURE:
PERIOD 1

1. Distribute Activity 1, *United States Population*. Explain that this table contains information that was collected about the age and sex of the United States Population as part of the 1990 Census of Population. Explain that the Constitution (Article I, Section II, Clause 3) requires that a **Census** be taken every ten years in order to determine each state's representation in Congress. Over the years Congress has authorized the collection of additional information to assist community organizations, businesses and industries, and agencies at all levels of government in their planning. Explain that the study of human population statistics is called *demography*, and demographic information is frequently used by both geographers and economists.

2. Discuss the information included in the table. Ask the students what the total population of the United States was in 1990 and how many were males and how many were females. (Total population was 248,709,873; 121,239,418 or 48.75% were males; and 127,470,455 or 51.25% were females.)

3. Ask the students to explain the entries for *Under 5* and *5–9 Years* (9,392,409 or 3.78% of the Total Population were males under 5 while 8,962,034 or 3.60% were females under 5. 9,262,527 or 3.72% of the Total Population were males between 5 and 9 years of age while 8,836,652 or 3.55% were females between 5 and 9 years of age).

4. Ask the students how they would determine how many males were between 10–14 years old. (Subtract 8,347,082—the number of females 10–14 years old from 17,114,249—the total number of persons 10–14 years old to get 8,767,167.) Continue for one or two more categories until you are confident that the students understand how to complete the MALE column on the chart.

5. Ask the students how they think the %MALE and %FEMALE columns were calculated.

(*Example:* 8,836,652 females between 5–9 years divided by 248,709,873 the total population = .0355 or 3.55%.) Calculate one or two of the missing percentages until you are confident that the students understand how to calculate the percentages.

6. Without explaining how to calculate **median age**, point out that half the males were 31.7 years of age or younger and half were 31.7 years of age or older while half the females were 34.1 years of age or younger and half were 34.1 years of age or older.

7. Display the transparency of Visual 1, *United States Population*, which is a completed version of Activity 1. After the students have had a chance to check their answers, ask the following questions:

- How old were you in 1990? (Most were probably in the 5–9 year age bracket.)

- What percentage of the total population was your age bracket? (7.27%—add 3.72 %MALE and 3.55 %FEMALE.)

- Which age brackets were a larger percentage of the population than your age bracket? (20–24 years, 25–29 years, 30–34 years, 35–39 years.)

- When were these groups born? (1966–1970, 1961–1965, 1956–1960, and 1951–1955, respectively; 1951–1970 collectively.)

- Which products and services do you think had increased demand during the decades of the 1950s and 1960s? (Diapers, baby food, strollers, etc.; children's clothing, bicycles, toys; medical care for expectant mothers and children; housing; baby-sitting services; etc.)

- Which expenditures did state and local governments increase dramatically from the mid-1950s through the mid-1970s? (Spending for new schools and teachers. During the late 1970s and 1980s, some schools were closed, retiring teachers were not replaced, and some teachers were laid off.)

8. Display the transparency of Visual 2, *United States Population Pyramid*. This is a population pyramid based on the data from Activity 1. Explain to the students that **population pyramids** are graphs that reveal the age and sex distribution of a region's population. These useful graphs can be compiled for neighborhoods, cities, states, and countries. One can even compare places with large populations with places with much smaller populations if percentages are used instead of numbers of persons. As you will see later, it is often useful to compare a community's population pyramid to the population pyramid of the United States. The graphs can be used to plan for new schools, marketing products, and providing social services. Population pyramids are standardized to always show male population on the left-hand side of the graph and female population on the right. Older age brackets are shown at the top of the graph and younger age brackets are at the bottom. Age groups are known as **cohorts**. Typically five-year age intervals are used. Use the population pyramid to review and reinforce answers to the questions in 7 above.

PERIOD 2

9. Have the students work in pairs or small groups. Place your better mathematics students where they can help students who might have difficulty. Provide each group with one of the four Activity 2 sheets. Ask them to complete the chart for ANYTOWN, SUBURBIA, OLDER CITY, or COLLEGE TOWN. When they have completed this task, provide a sheet of graph paper for them to create a population pyramid for the community. (You may want to review the description in 8 above and display the transparency of Visual 2, *United States Population Pyramid,* for the students to use as a guide. You may also want to check the accuracy of their answers or you may decide to provide answers before they create their population pyramids. Correct answers appear at the end of the lesson.)

10. Ask each group to write a paragraph explaining the shape of its graph, highlighting major findings (for example, many more males than females, large elderly population, large bulge in the late teens and early twenties' section of the graph). How does its community's pyramid differ from that of the United States as a whole?

CLOSURE

- Make transparencies of Visuals 3 through 6 which are population pyramids of Anytown, Suburbia, Older City, and College Town. Display them as the students report the findings they described in their paragraphs. Let the students see the different shapes and compare the population pyramids of each of the cities to the population pyramid of the United States. Then discuss likely demographic situations in the different places. ("Creative" explanations should be welcomed. This is the fun part of the lesson. ANYTOWN is a suburb of an older city with a number of families in their late twenties and thirties. The large number of females in their late teens and early twenties are students at a college which had only recently begun to admit men. SUBURBIA is an affluent suburb of a major city with a stable and aging population. OLDER CITY has a large immigrant population that was just beginning to arrive and raise families in 1990. The population bulge in the late teens through the twenties are the students at 7 colleges, universities, and professional schools. COLLEGE TOWN's name explains the bulge in the late teens and early twenties for both males and females, but what of the large number of males in their thirties and forties? In the United States as a whole, females outnumber males in every cohort beginning at age thirty. The answer—COLLEGE TOWN also has a state prison for men.)

- Discuss the potential business opportunities and the governmental services required in each community. This discussion should be used to motivate students for the extension activity. (You could spend an extra class having the students prepare lists of goods and services that might have a greater than average or lower than average demand in the community they worked with, using the population pyramids to support their hypotheses.)

EVALUATION

- Divide students into the same "town" groups used earlier in the lesson. Return their population pyramids, and ask them to discuss the distribution of the population in this town. Tell them to pretend they are residents of the town, and are representative of different age and gender groups. Ask them to assign roles to group members. Have each student write a paragraph about his or her life in this town.

EXTENSION ACTIVITY

The Bureau of the Census has published a *1990 Census of Population, General Population Characteristics* for each state in the union. The volume for your state is available from the Superintendent of Documents, U.S. Government Printing Office, Washington, DC 20402. Your public library probably has a copy. Table 61 contains the information your students will need to create a population pyramid for your community.

Once the data are collected and the graph has been produced, students may be assigned a number of projects. They can:

- explain the shape of your community's graph (what it looks like and how it is similar to or different from the United States as a whole).

- identify institutions or events that have had an impact on your community's population (for example, W.W. II; the Great Depression; a drought, flood, earthquake, or other natural disaster; a college; a military base; a large retirement community; a prison; a shopping mall; and the arrival or departure of a major employer).

- evaluate how your community's government meets the perceived needs of the various cohorts (for example, schools, community centers, parks, waste disposal, public health, police and fire protection, etc.). What are the major issues? Do various age groups take positions on these issues?

- predict the problems that your community may face in the future (for example, people moving away for economic reasons or in response to natural disasters, a growing or declining school-age population, crowding and urban blight, traffic congestion, and environmental contamination from old landfills) and how the

community might deal with such problems.

- recognize reasons why a new business might locate in your community or reasons why an existing business might leave your community?

These projects will require library research, interviews with businesspeople, government officials, or citizens in general, but they will be informed by an understanding of the composition of the community's population.

ACTIVITY 1
UNITED STATES POPULATION

Name _____

UNITED STATES POPULATION

	MALE	% MALE	FEMALE	% FEMALE	TOTAL
Under 5	9,392,409	3.78%	8,962,034	3.60%	18,354,443
5-9 Years	9,262,527	3.72%	8,836,652	3.55%	18,099,179
10-14 Years			8,347,082		17,114,249
15-19 Years			8,651,317		17,754,015
20-24 Years			9,344,716		19,020,312
25-29 Years			10,617,109		21,313,045
30-34 Years			10,985,954		21,862,887
35-39 Years			10,060,874		19,963,117
40-44 Years			8,923,802		17,615,786
45-49 Years			7,061,976		13,872,573
50-54 Years			5,835,775		11,350,513
55-59 Years			5,497,386		10,531,756
60-64 Years			5,669,120		10,616,167
65-69 Years			5,579,428		10,111,735
70-74 Years			4,585,517		7,994,823
75-79 Years			3,721,601		6,121,369
80-84 Years			2,567,645		3,933,739
85 Years and Over			2,222,467		3,080,165
TOTAL	121,239,418	48.75%	127,470,455	51.25%	248,709,873
Median Age	31.7		34.1		

Source: 1990 Census of Population, General Population Characteristics, United States, Table 16.

ACTIVITY 2A
ANYTOWN

Name _____

ANYTOWN

	MALE	% MALE	FEMALE	% FEMALE	TOTAL
Under 5	553	3.88%	541	3.79%	1,094
5-9 Years			495		980
10-14 Years			432		934
15-19 Years			830		1,400
20-24 Years			833		1,328
25-29 Years			647		1,236
30-34 Years			735		1,439
35-39 Years			667		1,285
40-44 Years			548		1,107
45-49 Years			418		826
50-54 Years			287		578
55-59 Years			260		488
60-64 Years			192		382
65-69 Years			206		373
70-74 Years			169		293
75-79 Years			146		226
80-84 Years			99		146
85 Years and Over			123		150
TOTAL	6,637	46.53%	7,628	53.47%	14,265
Median Age	31.0		30.6		

ACTIVITY 2B
SUBURBIA

Name _____

SUBURBIA

	MALE	% MALE	FEMALE	% FEMALE	TOTAL
Under 5	400	3.19%	379	3.02%	779
5-9 Years			368		710
10-14 Years			342		686
15-19 Years			390		817
20-24 Years			412		888
25-29 Years			360		770
30-34 Years			441		823
35-39 Years			478		928
40-44 Years			504		956
45-49 Years			474		900
50-54 Years			419		795
55-59 Years			408		790
60-64 Years			356		706
65-69 Years			379		678
70-74 Years			298		528
75-79 Years			248		388
80-84 Years			163		257
85 Years and Over			113		158
TOTAL	6,025	47.98%	6,532	52.02%	12,557
Median Age	37.5		40.9		

 From *Geography: Focus on Economics,* © National Council on Economic Education, New York, NY

ACTIVITY 2C
OLDER CITY

Name _____

OLDER CITY

	MALE	% MALE	FEMALE	% FEMALE	TOTAL
Under 5	6,432	3.79%	6,043	3.56%	12,475
5-9 Years			5,215		10,611
10-14 Years			4,550		9,250
15-19 Years			6,571		13,225
20-24 Years			8,652		17,626
25-29 Years			8,129		16,271
30-34 Years			7,454		15,082
35-39 Years			5,603		11,438
40-44 Years			4,793		9,479
45-49 Years			3,757		7,203
50-54 Years			3,444		6,299
55-59 Years			3,536		6,454
60-64 Years			3,901		7,159
65-69 Years			4,368		7,616
70-74 Years			4,190		6,922
75-79 Years			3,487		5,607
80-84 Years			2,504		3,676
85 Years and Over			2,695		3,466
TOTAL	80,867	47.61%	88,892	52.33%	169,859
Median Age	30.1		33.4		

ACTIVITY 2D
COLLEGE TOWN

Name _____

COLLEGE TOWN

	MALE	% MALE	FEMALE	% FEMALE	TOTAL
Under 5	639	3.01%	632	2.97%	1,271
5-9 Years			662		1,397
10-14 Years			576		1,229
15-19 Years			1,092		1,967
20-24 Years			1,304		2,745
25-29 Years			756		1,993
30-34 Years			806		2,055
35-39 Years			858		2,041
40-44 Years			720		1,683
45-49 Years			537		1,236
50-54 Years			339		768
55-59 Years			302		654
60-64 Years			285		562
65-69 Years			310		557
70-74 Years			245		436
75-79 Years			186		305
80-84 Years			145		221
85 Years and Over			105		129
TOTAL	11,389	53.60%	9,860	46.40%	21,249
Median Age	30.4		29.4		

ACTIVITY 2A-B
ANSWERS

ANYTOWN

	MALE	% MALE	FEMALE	% FEMALE	TOTAL
Under 5	553	3.88%	541	3.79%	1,094
5-9 Years	485	3.40%	495	3.47%	980
10-14 Years	502	3.52%	432	3.03%	934
15-19 Years	570	4.00%	830	5.82%	1,400
20-24 Years	495	3.47%	833	5.84%	1,328
25-29 Years	589	4.13%	647	4.54%	1,236
30-34 Years	704	4.94%	735	5.15%	1,439
35-39 Years	618	4.33%	667	4.68%	1,285
40-44 Years	559	3.92%	548	3.84%	1,107
45-49 Years	408	2.86%	418	2.93%	826
50-54 Years	291	2.04%	287	2.01%	578
55-59 Years	228	1.60%	260	1.82%	488
60-64 Years	190	1.33%	192	1.35%	382
65-69 Years	167	1.17%	206	1.44%	373
70-74 Years	124	0.87%	169	1.18%	293
75-79 Years	80	0.56%	146	1.02%	226
80-84 Years	47	0.33%	99	0.69%	146
85 Years and Over	27	0.19%	123	0.86%	150
TOTAL	6,637	46.53%	7,628	53.47%	14,265
Median Age	31.0		30.6		

SUBURBIA

	MALE	% MALE	FEMALE	% FEMALE	TOTAL
Under 5	400	3.19%	379	3.02%	779
5-9 Years	342	2.72%	368	2.93%	710
10-14 Years	344	2.74%	342	2.72%	686
15-19 Years	427	3.40%	390	3.11%	817
20-24 Years	476	3.79%	412	3.28%	888
25-29 Years	410	3.27%	360	2.87%	770
30-34 Years	382	3.04%	441	3.51%	823
35-39 Years	450	3.58%	478	3.81%	928
40-44 Years	452	3.60%	504	4.01%	956
45-49 Years	426	3.39%	474	3.77%	900
50-54 Years	376	2.99%	419	3.34%	795
55-59 Years	382	3.04%	408	3.25%	790
60-64 Years	350	2.79%	356	2.84%	706
65-69 Years	299	2.38%	379	3.02%	678
70-74 Years	230	1.83%	298	2.37%	528
75-79 Years	140	1.11%	248	1.97%	388
80-84 Years	94	0.75%	163	1.30%	257
85 Years and Over	45	0.36%	113	0.90%	158
TOTAL	6,025	47.98%	6,532	52.02%	12,557
Median Age	37.5		40.9		

ACTIVITY 2C-D
ANSWERS

OLDER CITY

	MALE	% MALE	FEMALE	% FEMALE	TOTAL
Under 5	6,432	3.79%	6,043	3.56%	12,475
5-9 Years	5,396	3.18%	5,215	3.07%	10,611
10-14 Years	4,700	2.77%	4,550	2.68%	9,250
15-19 Years	6,654	3.92%	6,571	3.87%	13,225
20-24 Years	8,974	5.29%	8,652	5.10%	17,626
25-29 Years	8,142	4.80%	8,129	4.79%	16,271
30-34 Years	7,628	4.49%	7,454	4.39%	15,082
35-39 Years	5,835	3.44%	5,603	3.30%	11,438
40-44 Years	4,586	2.70%	4,793	2.82%	9,479
45-49 Years	3,446	2.03%	3,757	2.21%	7,203
50-54 Years	2,855	1.68%	3,444	2.03%	6,299
55-59 Years	2,918	1.72%	3,536	2.08%	6,454
60-64 Years	3,258	1.92%	3,901	2.30%	7,159
65-69 Years	3,248	1.91%	4,368	2.57%	7,616
70-74 Years	2,732	1.61%	4,190	2.47%	6,922
75-79 Years	2,120	1.25%	3,487	2.05%	5,607
80-84 Years	1,172	0.69%	2,504	1.48%	3,676
85 Years and Over	771	0.45%	2,695	1.59%	3,466
TOTAL	80,867	47.61%	88,892	52.33%	169,859
Median Age	30.1		33.4		

COLLEGE TOWN

	MALE	% MALE	FEMALE	% FEMALE	TOTAL
Under 5	639	3.01%	632	2.97%	1,271
5-9 Years	735	3.46%	662	3.12%	1,397
10-14 Years	653	3.07%	576	2.71%	1,229
15-19 Years	875	4.12%	1,092	5.14%	1,967
20-24 Years	1,441	6.78%	1,304	6.14%	2,745
25-29 Years	1,237	5.82%	756	3.56%	1,993
30-34 Years	1,249	5.88%	806	3.79%	2,055
35-39 Years	1,183	5.57%	858	4.04%	2,041
40-44 Years	963	4.53%	720	3.39%	1,683
45-49 Years	699	3.29%	537	2.53%	1,236
50-54 Years	429	2.02%	339	1.60%	768
55-59 Years	352	1.66%	302	1.42%	654
60-64 Years	277	1.30%	285	1.34%	562
65-69 Years	247	1.16%	310	1.46%	557
70-74 Years	191	0.90%	245	1.15%	436
75-79 Years	119	0.56%	186	0.88%	305
80-84 Years	76	0.36%	145	0.68%	221
85 Years and Over	24	0.11%	105	0.49%	129
TOTAL	11,389	53.60%	9,860	46.40%	21,249
Median Age	30.4		29.4		

VISUAL 1
UNITED STATES POPULATION

UNITED STATES POPULATION

	MALE	% MALE	FEMALE	% FEMALE	TOTAL
Under 5	9,392,409	3.78%	8,962,034	3.60%	18,354,443
5-9 Years	9,262,527	3.72%	8,836,652	3.55%	18,099,179
10-14 Years	8,767,167	3.53%	8,347,082	3.36%	17,114,249
15-19 Years	9,102,698	3.66%	8,651,317	3.48%	17,754,015
20-24 Years	9,675,596	3.89%	9,344,716	3.76%	19,020,312
25-29 Years	10,695,936	4.30%	10,617,109	4.27%	21,313,045
30-34 Years	10,876,933	4.37%	10,985,954	4.42%	21,862,887
35-39 Years	9,902,243	3.98%	10,060,874	4.05%	19,963,117
40-44 Years	8,691,984	3.49%	8,923,802	3.59%	17,615,786
45-49 Years	6,810,597	2.74%	7,061,976	2.84%	13,872,573
50-54 Years	5,514,738	2.22%	5,835,775	2.35%	11,350,513
55-59 Years	5,034,370	2.02%	5,497,386	2.21%	10,531,756
60-64 Years	4,947,047	1.99%	5,669,120	2.28%	10,616,167
65-69 Years	4,532,307	1.82%	5,579,428	2.24%	10,111,735
70-74 Years	3,409,306	1.37%	4,585,517	1.84%	7,994,823
75-79 Years	2,399,768	0.96%	3,721,601	1.50%	6,121,369
80-84 Years	1,366,094	0.55%	2,567,645	1.03%	3,933,739
85 Years and Over	857,698	0.34%	2,222,467	0.89%	3,080,165
TOTAL	121,239,418	48.75%	127,470,455	51.25%	248,709,873
Median Age	31.7		34.1		

Source: 1990 Census of Population, General Population Characteristics, United States, Table 16.

From *Geography: Focus on Economics*, © National Council on Economic Education, New York, NY

VISUAL 2
UNITED STATES POPULATION

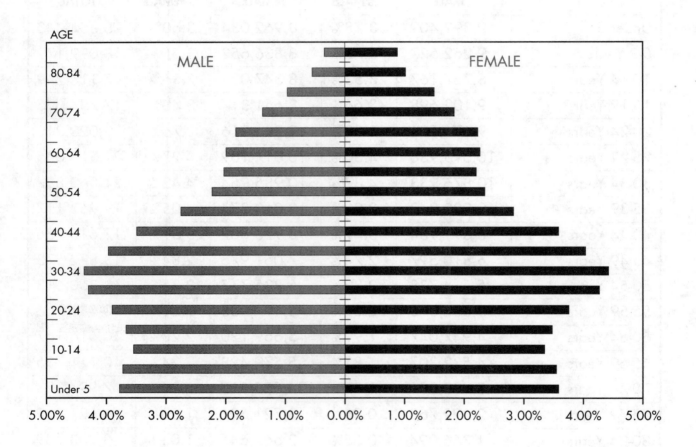

VISUAL 3
ANYTOWN

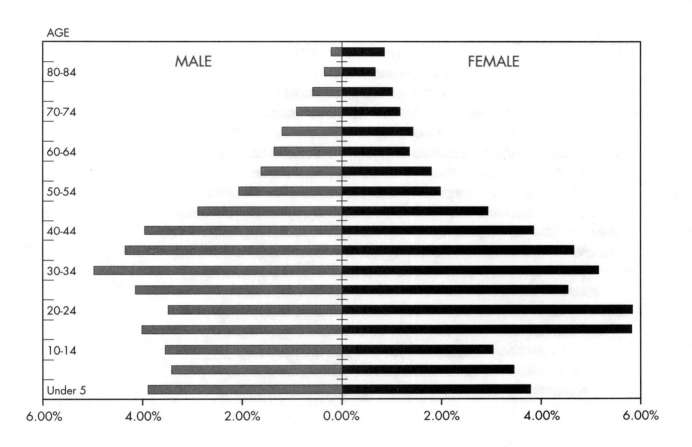

VISUAL 4
SUBURBIA

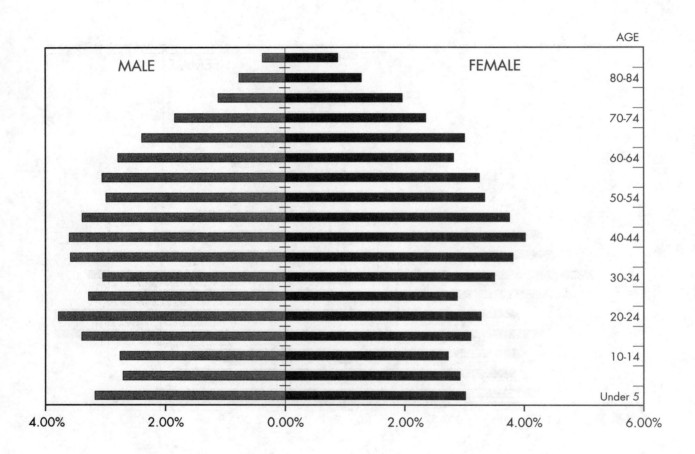

From *Geography: Focus on Economics,* © National Council on Economic Education, New York, NY

VISUAL 5
OLDER CITY

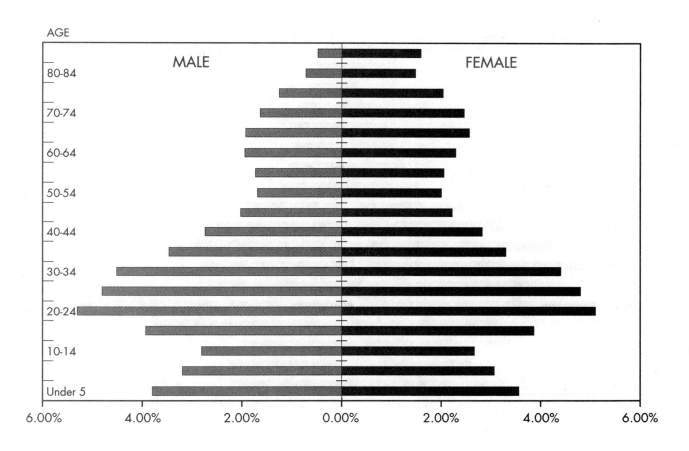

VISUAL 6
COLLEGE TOWN

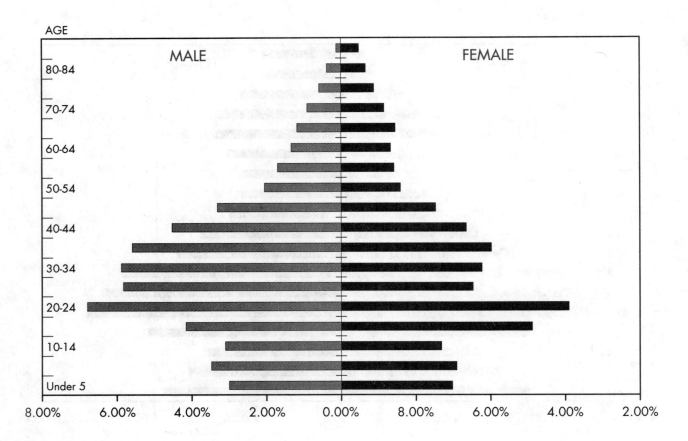

From *Geography: Focus on Economics*, © National Council on Economic Education, New York, NY

LESSON TEN
WHICH STATE IS THE LARGEST?

INTRODUCTION

Comparisons are important for economists and geographers. One useful tool for comparing the relative size of variables is the **cartogram**. A typical map showing country or state boundaries is a cartogram based on area.

Geographic and economic information can be acquired from cartograms, and cartograms can be used to display information in ways that help analysis. This activity uses cartograms to analyze data on area, population, and gross state product.

Population per square mile can be used as an approximation of **population density**. It is possible, however, to have densely populated cities in states that have vast areas of unoccupied territory.

Gross state product (GSP) is a measure of all output produced by economic activity within that state. It is analogous to the more familiar gross domestic product (GDP), the market value of all the goods and services produced in the nation's economy in a given year. **Gross state product per capita** is gross state product divided by the population of the state. It is each person's share of the gross state product if that product were to be divided equally among the people residing in the state. Gross state product per capita can be used as an approximation of economic well-being within a state.

The **population growth rate** for any year is the increase in population divided by the population at the beginning of that year, and it is expressed as a percent. The average annual population growth rate for any period of years is obtained by dividing the sum of the yearly growth rates by the number of years in the period. Population can grow if the number of births is greater than the number of deaths or the number of people immigrating is greater than the number of people emigrating. If these two sources of pop-

ulation growth are moving in opposite directions, the larger effect will determine the outcome.

CONCEPTS
Cartogram
Population Density
Gross State Product
Gross State Product Per Capita
Population Growth
Geographic Regions
Birth Rate
Death Rate
Immigration
Emigration

OBJECTIVES
◆ Recognize that the relative size of a region or state may be represented by its area, population, gross product, or other variables.

◆ Create population and gross state product cartograms.

◆ Acquire information from cartograms.

◆ Compare cartograms.

◆ Identify regions of high population density and low GSP per capita.

◆ Acquire information from tables.

◆ Hypothesize about reasons for different rates of population growth.

LESSON DESCRIPTION
Students create cartograms showing state populations and gross state products, then describe and analyze the results. Using Population Per Square Mile and Gross State Product Per Capita, they then identify regions of high population density and regions of low economic prosperity. Finally, they discuss factors that may help explain why particular states have high population growth rates.

TIME REQUIRED
Two class periods.

MATERIALS
One Transparency of Visual 1, *New England*

States Population Cartogram.
One copy for each student of
★ Activity 1, *Creating a Cartogram.*
One copy for each student of Activity 2, *State Population and Economic Statistics.*
A sheet of graph paper for each student.

PROCEDURE

1. Ask the class which is the largest state of the United States. (Most students will answer "Alaska.")

2. Then ask the students who answer "Alaska" how they have defined or qualified the concept "largest." (Answers will range from general measures of size to more precise measures like area in square miles.)

3. Make a list of other ways a state could be the largest. Suggest one or two if the class is slow to respond. (For example, a state could have the largest population, gross state product, percent of minority population, oil production, unemployment rate, or number of hazardous waste sites.)

4. Show the transparency of Visual 1, *New England States Population Cartogram.* Ask students how it differs from a map showing area in square miles. (Maine would be nearly four times the size of Massachusetts, New Hampshire and Vermont would be slightly larger than Massachusetts, Connecticut would be slightly larger and Rhode Island would be slightly smaller than they are shown in the cartogram.)

5. Distribute Activity 1, *Creating a Cartogram* and ask the class to read the explanation of how to create a cartogram. Answer any questions that students have about the process.

6. Divide the class into groups of two and assign each pair one of the following **geographic regions**:

A. New England: Maine, New Hampshire, Vermont, Massachusetts, Rhode Island, and Connecticut.

B. Middle Atlantic: New York, New Jersey, and Pennsylvania.

C. East North Central: Ohio, Indiana, Illinois, Michigan, and Wisconsin.

D. West North Central: Minnesota, Iowa, Missouri, North Dakota, South Dakota, Nebraska, and Kansas.

E. South Atlantic: Delaware, Maryland, District of Columbia, Virginia, West Virginia, North Carolina, South Carolina, Georgia, and Florida.

F. East South Central: Kentucky, Tennessee, Alabama, and Mississippi.

G. West South Central: Arkansas, Louisiana, Oklahoma, and Texas.

H. Mountain: Montana, Idaho, Wyoming, Colorado, New Mexico, Arizona, Utah, and Nevada.

I. Pacific: Washington, Oregon, California, Alaska, and Hawaii.

(The nine regions will involve only 18 students. You may choose to have more than one pair work on some of the regions, assign more than two students to the larger regions, or place students who may have difficulty with the activity with other students who may be able to help them.)

7. Distribute Activity 2, State Population and Economic Statistics.

Explain that Gross State Product is the dollar value of all the final goods and services produced by economic activity within a state during a year. One member of each group should create a cartogram showing Population (third column of Activity 2) and the other person should create a cartogram showing Gross State Product (fifth column of Activity 2). Tell the students to let one square on their population cartograms equal 100,000 persons and one square on their gross state product cartograms equal $1,000 million (1 billion). (This is essential for you to complete step 9 of this lesson.)

★ all students—basic course material
■ average and above average students
○ average and below average students

8. When the students have completed their cartograms, have them (using only their mental maps of the United States and the two cartograms they have created) report the *largest states* in each region. List the results.

ANSWERS:

REGION	SQUARE MILES	POPULATION	GROSS STATE PRODUCT
New England	Maine	Massachusetts	Massachusetts
Middle Atlantic	New York	New York	New York
East North Central	Michigan	Illinois	Illinois
West North Central	Minnesota	Missouri	Missouri
South Atlantic	Georgia	Florida	Florida
East South Central	Alabama	Tennessee	Tennessee
West South Central	Texas	Texas	Texas
Mountain	Montana	Arizona	Colorado
Pacific	Alaska	California	California

9. Combine the various regional cartograms to form a U.S. Population Cartogram and a U.S. Gross State Product Cartogram, posting them where students can see them, possibly on a wall or bulletin board. (It is not necessary to cut out the outlines of the cartograms. The regions will not fit together exactly in any case, so it's fine to have small spaces between the regions. Just place them geographically in their relative positions.)

- Using the *U.S. Population Cartogram*, point out that more than half of the people in the U.S. live in the nine most populous states. (California, New York, Texas, Florida, Pennsylvania, Illinois, Ohio, Michigan, and New Jersey.)

- Then using the *U.S. Gross State Product Cartogram*, show that the Gross State Product of the top nine states is more than half the Gross Domestic Product of the United States. (California, New York, Texas, Illinois, Pennsylvania, Florida, Ohio, New Jersey, and Michigan.)

- Suggest that students who don't trust their eyes and wish to verify these two statements can do the necessary calculations. (Using the data in Activity 2, *State Population and Economic Statistics*, the total population of the United States equals 258,181,000. The total population of the largest nine states equals 130,635,000. The

total of all of the Gross State Product is $5,161,671,000,000. The total of the Gross State Products of the top nine states equals $2,786,593,000,000.)

10. Ask how a cartogram of the United States showing the area in square miles of each state would differ from the cartograms of Population and Gross State Product. (During the discussion point out such contrasts as appear in the following table. Alaska, Montana, New Mexico, Arizona, Nevada, Colorado, Wyoming, and Oregon would be much larger on a cartogram showing area in square miles than they are on the population and gross state product cartograms. California would be slightly smaller on an area cartogram. Texas would be slightly larger.)

STATE	AREA RANK	POPULATION RANK	GROSS STATE PRODUCT RANK
Alaska	1	47	43
Texas	2	3	3
California	3	1	1
Montana	4	44	47
New Mexico	5	37	40
Arizona	6	23	26
Nevada	7	38	37
Colorado	8	26	24
Wyoming	9	51	51
Oregon	10	29	30

11. Tell the class that Population Per Square Mile (Column 4 of Activity 2, *State Population and Economic Statistics*) can be used as a rough estimate of population density. It is computed by dividing the state's population by the number of square miles in the state. Ask which regions of the United States are the most densely populated. (Southern part of New England, Middle Atlantic, northern part of South Atlantic.)

12. Tell the class that Gross State Product Per Capita (Column 6 of Activity 2, *State Population and Economic Statistics*) can be used as a rough measure of economic well-being. It is computed by dividing the state's gross state product by the state's population. In which regions of the U.S. are the states with GSP per capita below $16,000 located? (Mountain, West South Central, East South Central, South Atlantic, and West North Central.)

CLOSURE

- Have the students examine the data about Average Annual Population Growth rates from 1980–1990 (Column 7 of Activity 2, *State Population and Economic Statistics*). List the ten top states and their growth rates on the board.

STATE	POPULATION GROWTH RATE
Nevada	50.1%
Alaska	36.9%
Arizona	34.8%
Florida	32.7%
California	25.7%
New Hampshire	20.5%
Texas	19.4%
Georgia	18.6%
Utah	17.9%
Washington	17.8%

- What are some of the factors that help to determine the population of a state? (**Birth rate**: Column 8 of Activity 2, *State Population and Economic Statistics*; **death rate**: Column 9 of Activity 2, *State Population and Economic Statistics*; **immigration** into the state from other states or countries, and **emigration** from the state to other states or countries.)

- How might these factors be used to explain the population growth rates of the top ten states?

ANSWERS:

NEVADA: Gaming and tourism industries provide employment opportunities and the possibility of striking it rich, attracting people to the state. Nevada has a low cost of living and the eighth highest birth rate.

ALASKA: Developing oil and natural gas industries attracted many to the state. Alaska has the highest birth rate and the lowest death rate in the U.S.

ARIZONA: Climate is ideal for retirement and precision manufacturing. Thousands of high technology and aviation jobs were created in the early 1980s. There are large retail and service sectors. Arizona has the third highest birth rate and a below average death rate.

FLORIDA: Retirees and Hispanic (mostly Cuban and Latin American) immigrants have contributed to Florida's growing population. The space program, other high technology industries, the service sector, and tourism have provided jobs that have attracted others.

CALIFORNIA: Asian and Hispanic (mostly Mexican and Latin American) immigrants are a large part of California's growing population. Aerospace, entertainment, computers, banking, clothing and furniture manufacturing, and agriculture are major industries that attract people from other states. California is tied with Arizona for the third highest birth rate and has a below average death rate.

NEW HAMPSHIRE: High technology industries were attracted by New Hampshire's low taxes as were many individuals who commute to jobs in nearby states.

TEXAS: Hispanic (mostly Mexican) immigrants (legal and illegal) are a large part of Texas' growing population. Computers and other high technology industries and finance have attracted people from other states. Texas has the fourth highest birth rate and a below average death rate.

GEORGIA: The growth of old businesses like Coca Cola, a booming finance sector, and new electronic and aviation companies have brought many people to Georgia. Atlanta has become the hub of economic activity in the South. The Cable News Network (CNN) has made it a communications center as well. Georgia has the tenth highest birth rate.

UTAH: The growth of the Mormon faith has attracted people to Utah. United Parcel Service, J.C. Penney, and Novell are growing companies. Tourism is increasingly important. Utah has the second highest birth rate and the second lowest death rate.

WASHINGTON: The aerospace industry, especially Boeing, and white collar enterprises like MicroSoft provided opportunities that attracted people to Washington.

EVALUATION

- Tell the students to examine the population cartogram and the gross state product cartogram that have been displayed in the classroom. Ask each student to select two different states and write a paragraph describing how these states are alike or different and how they compare with the rest of the country.

- Ask the students to use an atlas with political, topographical, physical, and other maps of their state. How does the information provided by these maps help to explain the size of their state on the population and gross state product cartograms?

EXTENSION ACTIVITIES

1. Use a copy of the most recent *Statistical Abstract of the United States* to obtain data on state employment. Table 626 provides data on the total number of persons employed in each state and the number of these persons who are female. Some students can create cartograms based on each of these statistics.

Others can use the data on the unemployment rates for males and females found in the same table for their cartograms. Students should then write five statements describing their cartograms and offer a possible economic cause or consequence for each of their statements. (In order to make the task manageable, students should graph each of the nine regions, described in step 6 of the lesson, on a separate sheet of paper. This will also allow students to work together on this activity.)

2. Use a copy of the most recent *Statistical Abstract of the United States* to obtain data on housing. Table 1239 includes the lower quartile value, median value, and upper quartile value for owner-occupied housing units. Students can create cartograms for each of these statistics. They can then compare the values for their own state with those of the other states in their region and offer an economic explanation for the similarities

and differences they find. (In order to make the task manageable, students should graph each of the nine regions described in step 6 of the lesson, on a separate sheet of paper. This will also allow students to work together on this activity.)

VISUAL 1
NEW ENGLAND STATES POPULATION CARTOGRAM

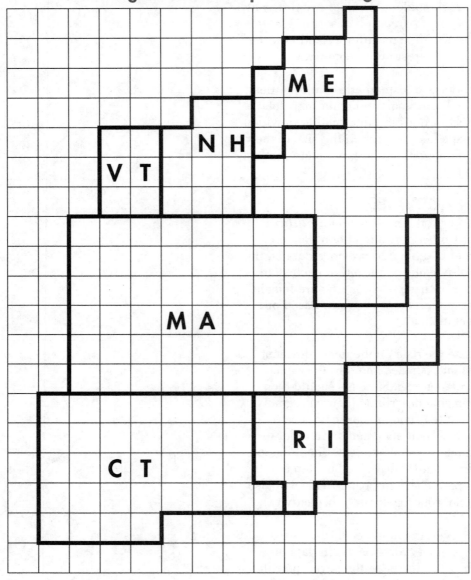

New England States Population Cartogram

1 Square = 100,000 Persons

ACTIVITY 1
CREATING A CARTOGRAM

Cartograms are maps that use population, gross domestic product, or some other characteristic to determine the size of an area. To construct a cartogram:

1. Find the highest and lowest values of the selected characteristic.

2. Decide on an appropriate value to assign to each square of the cartogram.

3. Determine how many squares will be needed for each area.

4. Remember to keep the relative location and shape of each area in mind when constructing the cartogram.

SAMPLE:

STATE	POPULATION (thousands)	ROUNDED POPULATION	NO. OF SQUARES NEEDED*
Maine	1,235	1,200	12
New Hampshire	1,105	1,100	11
Vermont	567	600	6
Massachusetts	5,996	6,000	60
Rhode Island	1,004	1,000	10
Connecticut	3,291	3,300	33

*Each square equals 100,000 persons

ACTIVITY 1 (continued)

New England States Population Cartogram

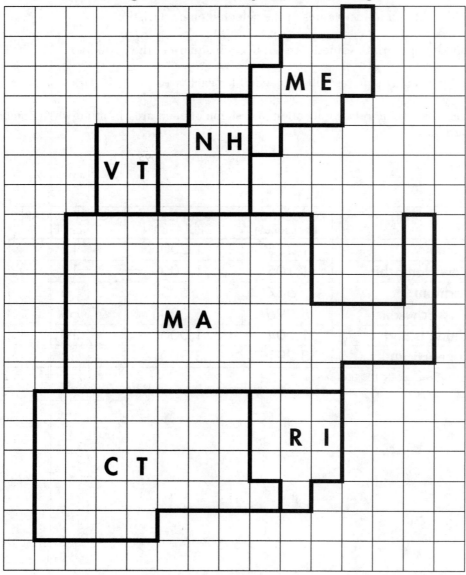

1 Square = 100,000 Persons

ACTIVITY 2
STATE POPULATION AND ECONOMIC STATISTICS

Column 1	Column 2	Column 3	Column 4	Column 5	Column 6	Column 7	Column 8	Column 9
STATE	AREA SQ. MILES	POPULATION (Thousands)	POPULATION PER SQ. MILE	GROSS STATE PRODUCT (GSP) (Million $)	GSP PER CAPITA	% AVERAGE ANNUAL POP. GROWTH 1980-1990	BIRTH RATE PER 1000 POPULATION	DEATH RATE PER 1000 POPULATION
Alabama	51,705	4,089	79.1	67,886	16,602	3.8	14.6	9.5
Alaska	591,000	570	1.0	19 582	34,354	36.9	21.4	3.9
Arizona	114,000	3,750	32.9	65,306	17,415	34.8	18.8	7.9
Arkansas	53,187	2,372	44.6	37,169	15,670	2.8	14.6	10.4
California	158,706	30,380	191.4	697,381	22,955	25.7	18.8	7.6
Colorado	104,091	3,377	32.4	66,180	19,597	14.0	16.2	6.5
Connecticut	5,018	3,291	655.8	88,863	27,002	5.8	14.9	8.8
Delaware	2,045	680	332.5	15,418	22,674	12.1	15.8	8.7
D.C.	69	598	8,666.7	39,363	65,824	– 4.9	17.1	12.4
Florida	58,664	13,277	226.3	226,964	17,095	32.7	14.9	10.6
Georgia	58,910	6,623	112.4	129,776	19,595	18.6	16.7	8.1
Hawaii	6,471	1,135	175.4	25,755	22,692	14.9	17.3	5.5
Idaho	83,564	1,039	12.4	13,339	12,836	6.7	15.7	7.7
Illinois	56,345	11,543	204.9	256,478	22,219	0.0	15.9	9.1
Indiana	36,185	5,610	155.0	105,314	18,773	1.0	14.7	9.0
Iowa	56,275	2,795	49.7	52,574	18,810	– 4.7	13.5	9.8
Kansas	82,277	2,495	30.3	48,829	19,571	4.8	15.5	9.2
Kentucky	40,410	3,713	91.9	65,858	17,737	0.7	13.7	9.6
Louisiana	47,752	4,252	89.0	79,138	18,612	0.3	16.8	8.5
Maine	33,265	1,235	37.1	23,474	19,007	9.2	14.3	9.6
Maryland	10,460	4,860	464.6	99,074	20,386	13.4	16.4	8.4
Massachusetts	8,284	5,996	723.8	144,791	24,148	4.9	15.0	9.6
Michigan	58,527	9,368	160.1	181,827	19,409	0.4	15.1	8.7
Minnesota	84,402	4,432	52.5	93,559	21,110	7.3	15.5	8.2
Mississippi	47,689	2,592	54.4	38,135	14,713	2.1	16.1	9.5
Missouri	69,697	5,158	74.0	100,081	19,403	4.1	14.9	9.9
Montana	147,046	808	5.5	13,104	16,218	1.6	14.5	8.4
Nebraska	77,355	1,593	20.6	31,115	19,532	0.5	14.9	9.3
Nevada	110,561	1,284	11.6	27,960	21,776	50.1	17.1	8.0
New Hampshire	9,279	1,105	119.1	24,504	22,176	20.5	16.0	8.1
New Jersey	7,787	7,760	996.5	203,375	26,208	5.0	15.3	9.5
New Mexico	121,593	1,548	12.7	25,414	16,417	16.3	17.9	6.9
New York	49,108	18,058	367.7	441,068	24,425	2.5	15.7	9.8
North Carolina	52,669	6,737	127.9	130,085	19,309	12.7	15.0	8.9
North Dakota	70,702	635	9.0	11,231	17,687	– 2.1	15.1	8.5
Ohio	41,330	10,939	264.7	211,545	19,339	0.5	14.8	9.2
Oklahoma	69,919	4,175	59.7	52,342	12,537	4.0	14.6	9.3
Oregon	97,073	2,922	30.1	52,118	17,836	7.9	14.5	9.0
Pennsylvania	45,308	11,961	264.0	227,898	19,053	0.1	13.8	10.5
Rhode Island	1,212	1,004	828.4	18,807	18,732	5.9	14.3	9 8
South Carolina	31,113	3,560	114.4	60,150	16,896	11.7	15.9	8.5
South Dakota	77,116	703	9.1	11,135	15,839	0.8	15.7	9.2
Tennessee	42,144	4,953	117.5	92,267	18,629	6.2	14.4	9.4
Texas	266,807	17,349	65.0	340,057	19,601	19.4	18.0	7.3
Utah	85,899	1,770	20.6	28,135	15,895	17.9	21.3	5.5
Vermont	9,614	567	59.0	11,502	20,286	10.0	14.6	8.4
Virginia	40,767	6,286	154.2	136,497	21,714	15.7	15.5	7.9
Washington	68,139	5,018	73.6	96,233	19,178	17.8	15.6	7.8
West Virginia	24,232	1,801	74.3	27,922	15,504	– 8.0	11.6	10.6
Wisconsin	56,153	4,955	88.2	93,978	18,966	4.0	14.6	8.9
Wyoming	97,809	460	4.7	11,115	24,163	– 3.4	15.0	6.8

Source: *Pocket USA*, London: The Economist Books, 1993.

From *Geography: Focus on Economics*, © National Council on Economic Education, New York, NY

LESSON ELEVEN
THE LANCASTER LANDFILL

INTRODUCTION

This lesson places students in the middle of a complex problem like those many communities are now facing. Individuals, businesses, and governments made decisions in the past that are producing consequences today. The hypothetical Town of Lancaster has closed a landfill after nearly 40 years of dumping of the waste products of the town's households, businesses, and industries. A variety of **hazardous waste** products are contaminating groundwater and finding their way into a local river creating potential health problems for fish, animals, and humans.

Local, state, and federal government agencies are involved, but the lines of responsibility are blurred. This problem is given a low priority hazard rating by the Environmental Protection Agency. Unless the EPA reconsiders, the burden of the cleanup will fall to the State and the Town of Lancaster. The State will pick up 75% of the cost of remedial action, but Lancaster must pay the rest of the bill.

Businesses and industries that dumped the hazardous materials in the landfill are potentially responsible parties (PRPs) and may be taken to court to recover part of the cost, but litigation is slow and costly and many of the worst offenders are no longer operating. It is not clear who the responsible parties are nor whether they have assets sufficient to meet judgments made by the courts.

The citizens of Lancaster have several options. They can postpone action temporarily, wait until state or federal agencies or courts mandate action, or choose one of three courses of action. A Special Lancaster Town Meeting will choose.

This lesson illustrates the economic concept of **third party costs**, costs borne by those who are neither producers nor consumers of the product.

While it is not clear which specific products have produced the hazardous waste, at least some of the people incurring the costs have come to the community since the landfill was closed. Others neither included hazardous waste in their household trash nor worked for one of the companies that dumped the offending chemicals.

The lesson addresses a major geographic theme—the interaction of people and environments—especially the changes that technology produces and their positive and negative consequences.

CONCEPTS

Environment
Government Regulation
Hazardous Waste
Third Party Costs
Property Rights
Market Mechanism
Technology

OBJECTIVES

◆ Identify the problem that prompted government action in the case.

◆ Participate in a simulation according to an assigned role.

◆ Analyze the costs and benefits of proposed solutions and decide which decisions to support.

◆ Discuss the experience of the simulation and its positive and negative aspects.

◆ Hypothesize ways to avoid similar problems.

◆ Discuss alternatives that rely upon the market to "regulate" the environment.

LESSON DESCRIPTION

Students participate in a simulated town meeting called to consider proposed solutions to the problem of groundwater contamination. Hazardous waste accumulated in a landfill over many years is creating the problem. The landfill in no longer in use, but it poses a risk to fish, wildlife, and people living nearby. Each student is provided with a specific role and a point of view. While it is expected that some students may feel frustration if their favorite solution is not chosen, that experience may be useful when they discuss the merits of market solutions as alternatives to political solutions.

Following a brief discussion during which students debrief the simulation, the students are asked to consider ways in which the problem could have been avoided. Assuming that most of their suggestions will be forms of regulation, the teacher will introduce ways in which the market mechanism might be used.

TIME REQUIRED
Two or three class periods

MATERIALS
■ One copy of Activity 1, *Lancaster Landfill Simulation,* for each student.
★ One copy of Activity 2, *Role Cards*, to cut up and distribute to students.
One transparency of Visual 1, *Rules for Lancaster Town Meeting*, and several copies to post around the classroom.

PROCEDURE
1. Distribute Activity 1, *Lancaster Landfill Simulation,* to each student.

2. Cut up Activity 2, *Role Cards*. Assign the following roles to the students and give each student the card appropriate to her or his role.

- Town Meeting Moderator (This student must be able to control the class during the town meeting. If you don't have a student who can handle this role, you can serve as moderator.)
- Town Manager
- Selectmen (Choose 3)
- Public Works Director
- Owners of active businesses and industries (Choose 3)
- Owners of inactive businesses and industries (Choose 3)
- Environmental activists (Choose 5)
- Homeowners (Choose 3)
- Landlords (Choose 2)
- Tenants (Choose 4)
- Citizens (Rest of the class)

3. Allow time for the students to read the activity and think about their roles. If your students are not used to role playing, you may want to assign the roles the day before the simulation.

4. Briefly discuss Activity 1, *Lancaster Landfill Simulation,* and be sure the students understand the problem in Lancaster and what each of the three articles would do to remedy the problem.

5. Display the transparency of Visual 1, *Rules for Lancaster Town Meeting*, and go over the rules one at a time, answering questions as they come up. On the day of the simulation, post copies of the rules at strategic places in the classroom.

6. Allow the moderator to conduct the simulation. Observe and make notes about the students' behavior in their roles. (If you have to moderate the town meeting, you may want to tape record the debate, because it will be difficult to preside and take notes at the same time.)

7. Use your notes to discuss what took place in the simulation. Do not be surprised if the students express frustration with the inefficiency of the democratic process as a way to solve Lancaster's problem. This is a good opportunity to stress the importance of being informed about public issues as well as the costs of becoming informed. For example, in the real world the environmental activists, public officials, and the business owners would know more about the problem and have a clearer idea of their positions than your students.

CLOSURE
- Ask the students to suggest ways that the problem could have been avoided. (Anticipate that they will suggest a number of regulations that might have been enacted and enforced, and allow a few minutes to discuss each suggestion presented.)

- Suggest that the real problem is that when everybody owns something, nobody owns it. This is easy enough to see when talking about

★ all students–basic course material
■ average and above average students
○ average and below average students

95

the air, rivers, and oceans. When **property rights** are unspecified or the property is held in common, who has an incentive to maintain or improve its condition? While it is true that Lancaster owned the landfill, there was no incentive to restrict what was deposited in it until the problem became visible.

- Ask students to think about a landfill, which would accept hazardous waste but charge a fee sufficient to dispose of the waste safely. That fee would then be a cost of doing business. It is likely that the price of the product would increase and the quantity sold would decrease. As the landfill space became more scarce relative to the demand for its use, the fee would be increased. In some places a form of this system is in place. Ask students if they or their families have paid a hazardous waste fee to a garage to dispose of discarded tires or used oil.

- Once students have accepted the special hazardous waste fee, suggest that landfills might be owned by private citizens. If people living next to the landfill could recover triple damages for contamination of their property, couldn't private landfill owners be trusted to charge a fee high enough to maintain safe landfills? Wouldn't these high fees cause businesses to reduce their hazardous waste or their production?

EVALUATION

- Ask students to choose an outcome that might have happened in Lancaster, and write a paragraphs about how this changed the lives of their characters in the town meeting simulation.

- Divide students into cooperative groups and tell them to pretend that they are members of a special town committee formed to improve environmental safety in Lancaster. Ask them to discuss the rules or restrictions that they may or may not need to pass to improve the situation in Lancaster. Have each group member write down the suggestion he or she thinks is best and why.

- Discuss with students incidents of pollution

that have occurred in their community or state. Ask them who the parties were and what the issues were in each situation. Have students write letters to public officials expressing their views on the issues and urging what they believe would be appropriate action.

EXTENSION

1. Project assignment: Ask students to collect pictures (minimum of 5, maximum of 10) from magazines (*National Geographic, Time, Life, Newsweek, U.S. News and World Report*) that depict people interacting with the environment. For each picture they should indicate:

- the nature of the interaction.

- the reasons for the interaction.

- how the interaction has changed the environment.

- the different perceptions that people have of environmental changes.

- how the environmental changes may influence other people and places.

ACTIVITY 1
LANCASTER LANDFILL SIMULATION

THE ISSUE

The problem was identified during a routine inspection of the landfill while it was still in operation. A large pond had formed where the trash had dammed a stream that fed into the local river. The inspector was alarmed by the bright orange color of the water. It took the town of Lancaster three years to arrange for another way to dispose of their trash before they could close the landfill.

That was not the end of the problem. Residents complained to local officials about "foul" odors coming from the landfill. They expressed concern about their children's safety when playing near the river. When the orange stains on their children's clothing did not come off after repeated washings, they feared for their children's health.

The town contacted the state environmental agency. After review of the landfill inspection, the state agency listed the site for further investigation and sent a request for a federal Environmental Protection Agency (EPA) investigation. The state then did its own study to identify health risks to town residents and to gather information to help decide how to solve the problem. The state regulators also hoped to find evidence that would be used to convince the EPA that the federal government should get involved.

The EPA investigated the problem. The investigators conducted a site inspection and gave the site a low priority hazard ranking that left further action up to the State.

STATE STUDY SUMMARY

This investigation revealed much groundwater contamination. Hazardous substances were found in the water, sediment, soil, gas, and atmosphere in and around the site. Some of the substances that endangered human health were:

- volatile compounds such as benzene, vinal chloride, and naphthalene found in solvents, petroleum products, dyes, and paints.

- metals, including arsenic, cadmium, chromium, lead, and mercury.

Benzene and vinal chloride are known to cause cancer. The metals are known to become concentrated in fish and waterfowl. People could be exposed to danger by direct contact with the contaminated water and sediments or by eating fish or waterfowl from the nearby river. Young children might fall into the water and accidentally swallow some.

POSSIBLE REMEDIES

- Fencing in the site to reduce risk of human exposure at a cost of $100,000.

- Recapping the landfill to reduce the danger of the hazardous substances coming to the surface. This would include a clay cap, a vent system, a system to divert water away from the landfill, a liner, sand for drainage, top soil, and vegetative cover at an average cost of $100,000 per acre for approximately 33 acres. The cost will be higher if the source of clay is far away from the site.

- Recapping the landfill and installing clay walls around the landfill and a system of wells that will contain gas and water to the site in order to prevent the hazardous substances from spreading underground to other sites and into nearby streams. This system will cost between $10–20 million, depending on the depth to bedrock and the size of the wall and well system. It will cost $10 million if the system is installed only where the problem is now occurring. It will cost $20 million if it is put around the entire landfill site.

The state will pay for 100% of the investigation costs and 75% of the repair costs unless the EPA picks up some or all of the costs. Both the state and the EPA will try to find potentially responsible parties (PRPs).

ACTIVITY 1 (continued)

The town of Lancaster will be responsible for 25% of the repair costs. It will be more difficult to find PRPs because of the large legal fees.

SETTING FOR THE SIMULATION

Lancaster is a town of just under 20,000 residents. Its form of government is a representative town meeting. A special town meeting has been called to consider three possible responses to the landfill problem. The warrant for the meeting has three items to be debated and voted upon:

1. An article authorizing the Director of Public Works of the Town of Lancaster to begin the steps required to recap the landfill, install clay walls and wells around the landfill and authorizing the Town Manager and the Board of Selectmen to let the contracts necessary to do this and to file the necessary papers with the State Environmental Agency to receive 75% reimbursement for the cost of the project. Estimated cost of the project: $16,000,000; estimated cost to the Town of Lancaster: $4,000,000, to be financed by selling municipal bonds with a term of 30 years.

2. An article authorizing the Director of Public Works of the Town of Lancaster to begin the steps required to recap the landfill and authorizing the Town Manager and the Board of Selectmen to let the contracts necessary to do this and to file the necessary papers with the State Environmental Agency to receive 75% reimburse-ment for the cost of the project. Estimated cost of the project: $3,200,000; estimated cost to the Town of Lancaster: $800,000, to be financed by selling municipal bonds with a term of 10 years.

3. An article authorizing the Director of Public Works of the Town of Lancaster to begin the steps required to fence in the landfill and authorizing the Town Manager and the Board of Selectmen to let the contracts necessary to do this. Estimated cost of the project: $100,000; estimated cost to the Town of Lancaster: $100,000, to be financed with this year's tax revenues.

If the first article is adopted by the town meeting, articles 2 and 3 will not be considered. If the second article is adopted, article 3 will not be considered.

ACTIVITY 2
ROLE CARDS

Town Meeting Moderator: You will preside as described above, but you will not participate in the debate or vote on the articles.

Town Manager: You are most concerned about the costs of the various proposals. You have other programs that you feel are more important. (Be creative!) While you admit that some chronic conditions may have been aggravated by living near the landfill, there are no documented serious health problems.

Selectman #1: You distrust experts and find it difficult to understand the scientific studies and the need for so much money to deal with the problem. You don't want to impose a large debt on a community whose industrial base is shrinking.

Selectman #2: You distrust experts and find it difficult to understand the scientific studies and the need for so much money to deal with the problem. You don't want to impose a large debt on a community whose industrial base is shrinking.

Selectman #3: You distrust experts and find it difficult to understand the scientific studies and the need for so much money to deal with the problem. You don't want to impose a large debt on a community whose industrial base is shrinking.

Lancaster Public Works Director: You are close to retirement and would prefer that nothing be done about the problem while you are still in charge.

Active Lancaster Business and Industry Owner #1: Most of the hazardous materials were dumped by industries. Because you provided most of the waste stream, you may be legally responsible for much of the cost of the cleanup. However, there may be long legal battles before the courts make a decision. In addition, your taxes will increase if the town votes to remedy the situation. You fear you may be forced to close your business if the costs are too high, and that would mean the loss of jobs for residents of the town.

Active Lancaster Business and Industry Owner #2: Most of the hazardous materials were dumped by industries. Because you provided most of the waste stream, you may be legally responsible for much of the cost of the cleanup. However, there may be long legal battles before the courts make a decision. In addition, your taxes will increase if the town votes to remedy the situation. You fear you may be forced to close your business if the costs are too high, and that would mean the loss of jobs for residents of the town.

ACTIVITY 2 (continued)

Active Business and Industry Owner #3: Most of the hazardous materials were dumped by industries. Because you provided most of the waste stream, you may be legally responsible for much of the cost of the cleanup. However, there may be long legal battles before the courts make a decision. In addition, your taxes will increase if the town votes to remedy the situation. You fear you may be forced to close your business if the costs are too high, and that would mean the loss of jobs for residents of the town.

Former Business and Industry Owner #1: You received much of the benefit of the landfill, so you may be responsible for the cost of the cleanup. Because your business is no longer operating, you will be harder to identify and locate. You expect long legal battles before the courts make a decision. You have very little of value that the courts could make you use to pay fines or to pay for the cleanup.

Former Business and Industry Owner #2: You received much of the benefit of the landfill, so you may be responsible for the cost of the cleanup. Because your business is no longer operating, you will be harder to identify and locate. You expect long legal battles before the courts make a decision. You have very little of value that the courts could make you use to pay fines or to pay for the cleanup.

Former Business and Industry Owner #3: You received much of the benefit of the landfill, so you may be responsible for the cost of the cleanup. Because your business is no longer operating, you will be harder to identify and locate. You expect long legal battles before the courts make a decision. You have very little of value that the courts could make you use to pay fines or to pay for the cleanup.

Environmental Activist #1: The local environmental groups you belong to picked up on the complaints of residents and pressed for action by town officials. Particularly important was an interview with the president of the largest environmental organization, which was aired on network television. You prefer Article 1, but you will support the most complete plan that can get the necessary support to pass.

Environmental Activist #2: The local environmental groups you belong to picked up on the complaints of residents and pressed for action by town officials. Particularly important was an interview with the president of the largest environmental organization, which was aired on network television. You prefer Article 1, but you will support the most complete plan that can get the necessary support to pass.

Environmental Activist #3: The local environmental groups you belong to picked up on the complaints of residents and pressed for action by town officials. Particularly important was an interview with the president of the largest environmental organization, which was aired on network television. You prefer Article 1, but you will support the most complete plan that can get the necessary support to pass.

Environmental Activist #4: The local environmental groups you belong to picked up on the complaints of residents and pressed for action by town officials. Particularly important was an interview with the president of the largest environmental organization, which was aired on network television. You prefer Article 1, but you will support the most complete plan that can get the necessary support to pass.

From *Geography: Focus on Economics*, © National Council on Economic Education, New York, NY

ACTIVITY 2 (continued)

Environmental Activist #5: The local environmental groups you belong to picked up on the complaints of residents and pressed for action by town officials. Particularly important was an interview with the president of the largest environmental organization which was aired on network television. You prefer Article 1, but you will support the most complete plan that can get the necessary support to pass.

Homeowner #1 near the site: You are suffering from the health hazards and the value of your property is going down. You would like to move, but you are having difficulty finding buyers at any price. You want the problem solved by adoption of article 1 or 2.

Homeowners #2 near the site: You are suffering from the health hazards and the value of your property is going down. You would like to move, but you are having difficulty finding buyers at any price. You want the problem solved by adoption of article 1 or 2.

Homeowner #3 near the site: You are suffering from the health hazards and the value of your property is going down. You would like to move, but you are having difficulty finding buyers at any price. You want the problem solved by adoption of article 1 or 2.

Landlord #1 near the site: Many of your tenants have moved out, and it has been hard to rent your apartments. If the site is cleaned up, your property will increase in value, and you can raise your rents.

Landlord #2 near the site: Many of your tenants have moved out, and it has been hard to rent your apartments. If the site is cleaned up, your property will increase in value, and you can raise your rents.

Tenant #1 near the site: You are not sure how great a risk your family is taking by living so close to the site, but you are very worried about your children. You haven't been able to find other housing with rents you can afford, and you are afraid that you won't be able to pay increased rents.

Tenant #2 near the site: You are not sure how great a risk your family is taking by living so close to the site, but you are very worried about your children. You haven't been able to find other housing with rents you can afford, and you are afraid that you won't be able to pay increased rents.

ACTIVITY 2 (continued)

Tenant #3 near the site: You are not sure how great a risk your family is taking by living so close to the site, but you are very worried about your children. You haven't been able to find other housing with rents you can afford, and you are afraid that you won't be able to pay increased rents.

Tenant #4 near the site: You are not sure how great a risk your family is taking by living so close to the site, but you are very worried about your children. You haven't been able to find other housing with rents you can afford, and you are afraid that you won't be able to pay increased rents.

Citizen #1: You know that you benefited from lower trash disposal costs for up to 35 or 40 years while the landfill was still operating, but you realize that most of the hazardous materials were dumped by industries. You will have to pay increased taxes to fund whatever is done, and you want to see that taxpayers' money is not wasted. You are looking for the least expensive but effective solution.

Citizen #2: You know that you benefited from lower trash disposal costs for up to 35 or 40 years while the landfill was still operating, but you realize that most of the hazardous materials were dumped by industries. You will have to pay increased taxes to fund whatever is done, and you want to see that taxpayers' money is not wasted. You are looking for the least expensive but effective solution.

Citizen #3: You know that you benefited from lower trash disposal costs for up to 35 or 40 years while the landfill was still operating, but you realize that most of the hazardous materials were dumped by industries. You will have to pay increased taxes to fund whatever is done, and you want to see that taxpayers' money is not wasted. You are looking for the least expensive but effective solution.

Citizen #4: You know that you benefited from lower trash disposal costs for up to 35 or 40 years while the landfill was still operating, but you realize that most of the hazardous materials were dumped by industries. You will have to pay increased taxes to fund whatever is done, and you want to see that taxpayers' money is not wasted. You are looking for the least expensive but effective solution.

Citizen #5: You know that you benefited from lower trash disposal costs for up to 35 or 40 years while the landfill was still operating, but you realize that most of the hazardous materials were dumped by industries. You will have to pay increased taxes to fund whatever is done, and you want to see that taxpayers' money is not wasted. You are looking for the least expensive but effective solution.

Citizen #6: You know that you benefited from lower trash disposal costs for up to 35 or 40 years while the landfill was still operating, but you realize that most of the hazardous materials were dumped by industries. You will have to pay increased taxes to fund whatever is done, and you want to see that taxpayers' money is not wasted. You are looking for the least expensive but effective solution.

VISUAL 1
RULES FOR LANCASTER TOWN MEETING

1. You have been assigned a role for the Lancaster Town Meeting. You are to represent your position faithfully, but you are encouraged to listen to the arguments presented by others and vote as you think you would if the simulation were real life. You are to use your own last names.

2. The Town Meeting Moderator will call the meeting to order, read and move the adoption of each article in turn, recognize people who wish to speak, and maintain proper decorum in the meeting.

3. If you are recognized by the Town Moderator, you may speak to the question being debated.

4. You are not to address any person except the Town Moderator directly. She or he is to be referred to as **the Chair**.

5. If you refer to what another person has said, say "I agree (disagree) with what Mr. _____ or Ms. _____ proposes because..."

6. You must come to the front of the room to speak. If you speak out or violate any of the procedures described above, you will be ruled **out of order** by the Chair, and you will have to sit down.

7. The Town Manager and Selectmen will be asked to state their position on the articles before the Town Meeting members begin debate.

8. Debate on each article will continue until those who desire to speak have had their opportunity. If people begin to repeat themselves or the debate seems to be over, the Chair will ask, "Are you ready for a vote?" If she or he judges that there is a clear majority ready, the Chair will call for a standing vote and ask one or two people to help count the vote. The Chair will then announce the result and if a majority have supported the article, she or he will say, "The article is adopted." Otherwise, the Chair will say, "The article is not adopted." Then the Chair will read and move the adoption of the next article.

LESSON TWELVE
GEO-POEMS AND ECO-POEMS

INTRODUCTION

There are many ways to organize and present geographic and economic information. Maps, graphs, illustrations, diagrams, charts, tables, spreadsheets, and timelines are frequently used to complement and enrich oral and written narrative reports. Creativity is an important aspect in the creation of such aids to understanding. In addition to these more traditional forms, poems, collages, plays, journals, photo essays, and multimedia presentations can be both effective and satisfying means of communicating one's ideas. This activity uses poems and other visual elements to capture the essence of the student's understanding of a place.

CONCEPTS

Location
Place
Human-Environment Interaction
Movement
Regions
Resources
Economic Institutions
Role of Government

(None of these concepts is taught in this lesson. If students have not completed the other lessons in this publication, they should refer to the definitions in the Glossary.)

OBJECTIVES

◆ Write a Geo-Poem or an Eco-Poem about a city or country.

◆ Share poems with classmates.

◆ Recognize differences between geographic and economic perspectives.

◆ Evaluate the merits of knowing a place through poetry and other less traditional forms of communication.

LESSON DESCRIPTION

Students write a Geo-Poem (pronounced jē̄ō pō̄əm) or an Eco-Poem (pronounced ĕkō pō̄əm) describing a city or country, share their poems in small groups, select the best poem in each group to share with the class, discuss differences between geographic and economic perspectives, and evaluate this activity as a way of learning.

TIME REQUIRED

Two or more class periods. (The poem may be assigned as homework for several days.)

MATERIALS

★ One copy of Activity 1, *GEO-POEM*, for half the students.

★ One copy of Activity 2, *ECO-POEM*, for half the students.

PROCEDURE

1. Tell the class that the purpose of this lesson is to help them understand how a geographic perspective and an economic perspective can be used to understand a place.

2. Divide the class into groups of two or let the students choose their own partners. You may want to pair more able students with less able students. They may be able to help each other in this kind of activity. Let each pair decide whether they will work together on both poems or work alone on one of the poems.

3. Distribute Activity 1, *GEO-POEM*, and Activity 2, *ECO-POEM*, to each pair of students. Review the directions and discuss the sample poems with the students. Decide beforehand whether you will assign specific places for them to write about, restrict the places to those that have been studied in class, or leave the choice of place to them.

4. When the students have completed the activity, divide them into small discussion groups of 4 to 6 students. Ask them to share their poems within their groups by reading them aloud. (If your students will be uncomfortable with this, omit steps 4 and 5. You may want to select poems to read or display for the class.)

★ all students–basic course material
■ average and above average students
○ average and below average students

5. Ask the groups to share one of their poems with the class. If time permits, ask each group to share a second poem.

CLOSURE

Ask the students to consider the following questions:

- How does a geographic perspective differ from an economic perspective? (Possible answers: A geographic perspective includes a greater concern for physical processes and systems that shape the earth's surface. An economic perspective includes a greater concern for the ways resources are used to produce the goods and services that consumers want and how those goods and services are distributed. Keep in mind that the purpose of this discussion is to ascertain the differences that students perceive following this lesson.)

- What did you learn from writing poems about places? How did this lesson compare with other geography or economics lessons? (Use this discussion to identify students who enjoy more artistic forms of expression.)

EVALUATION

- Assign each student a city or a country that the class has studied. Allow the students to write Geo-Poems or Eco-Poems, draw or paint pictures, write stories or essays, or create posters that capture what their assigned places mean to them. (If you know that a student has artistic talent in another area such as music or producing multimedia presentations, or if a student has another creative suggestion, be flexible!)

EXTENSION ACTIVITIES

- Students who enjoyed this lesson may want to prepare a collection of Geo-Poems and Eco-Poems that describe cities and countries from several different regions.

- Students who found it difficult to write poetry may be better able to express themselves through drawings, paintings, or collages. Ask them to include all the elements from a Geo-Poem or an Eco-Poem in creations about their favorite cities or countries.

- Newspaper and periodical articles, maps, charts, tables, illustrations, graphs, and diagrams can be used to create scrapbooks illustrating geographic and economic perspectives. The information gathered in such scrapbooks can be the beginning of more ambitious research reports.

ACTIVITY 1
GEO-POEM

This activity can help you put together what you know about a place or region and express it in a creative way. Start with a particular place, such as a city (Nairobi) and end with the country (Kenya) or start with the country (Kenya) and end with the region (East Africa).

Use adjectives and word pictures as you write. The Geo-Poem (pronounced jēō pōəm) is *not* a formula but a way to help you organize your thoughts before you write. Try to capture the essence, the spirit, and the character of the place you write about. You can create your poem individually or in pairs.

Line 1 City or country name.

Line 2 Four physical features that describe this place.

Line 3 Three cultural features.

Line 4 *Neighbor of* or *bordering*.

Line 5 Description of climate (temperature and precipitation) in a season or year.

Line 6 *Home of* three items that give the place character.

Line 7 Three events or historical trends that have shaped this place.

Line 8 Two issues or problems of the place.

Line 9 Country or region name.

OPTIONAL

When the poem is written, draw a country or region outline of the place on colored paper, then cut it out and mount the outline on larger oak tag. Write the Geo-Poem on the outline of the country or region. Decorate the borders with small pictures, symbols, or diagrams of the place to add a visual dimension.

SAMPLE GEO-POEM

MOROCCO

Morocco.

Bounded by the Atlas Mountains, Mediterranean shore, encroaching deserts, and a rugged Atlantic coast,

Her people speak Arabic, French, Spanish, and the dialects of nomadic Berber herdsmen; most share a Sunni Muslim faith.

Algeria lies beyond the mountains; Mauritania, challenger to her claim to the Western Sahara, is farther south; and Spain is within eyesight across the Strait of Gibraltar.

Coastal dwellers bask in her Mediterranean climate of warm winters and comfortable summers while others *enjoy* her hot arid deserts and snowcapped mountains.

Berbers, Arabs, and Europeans, surrounded by traditional Islamic architecture, design, and art, populate old and new cities—Marrakesh, Fez, Tangier, Rabat and Casablanca—each has a distinctive history and personality.

Shaped by centuries of struggle between invading Arab and resident Berber cultures; she has absorbed the languages, political, economic, and social institutions of Portuguese, Spanish, and French traders and colonizers; while she has evolved into a constitutional monarchy, uniting church and state in the person of the King.

Large numbers of uneducated young men migrate to urban centers seeking nonexistent jobs while educated young women already living there wrestle with conflicts between their modern ideas and Islam's traditional roles for women.

Morocco, Pearl of North Africa.

ACTIVITY 2
ECO-POEM

This activity can help you put together what you know about a place or region and express it in a creative way. Start with a particular place, such as a city (Nairobi) and end with the country (Kenya) or start with the country (Kenya) and end with the region (East Africa).

Use adjectives and word pictures as you write. The Eco-Poem (pronounced ĕkō pōəm) is *not* a formula but a way to help you organize your thoughts before you write. Try to capture the essence, the spirit, and the character of the place you write about. You can create your poem individually or in pairs.

Line 1 City or country name.

Line 2 Four abundant resources of this place.

Line 3 Three economic activities.

Line 4 Major trading partner(s).

Line 5 Type of economy and/or government.

Line 6 *Home of* three economic landmarks.

Line 7 Three events or historical trends that have shaped this place.

Line 8 Two economic issues or problems of current importance.

Line 9 Country or region name.

OPTIONAL

When the poem is written, draw a country or region outline of the place on colored paper, then cut it out and mount the outline on larger oak tag. Write the Geo-Poem on the outline of the country or region. Decorate the borders with small pictures, symbols, or diagrams of the place to add a visual dimension.

SAMPLE ECO-POEM

BOSTON

Boston.

Renowned for succulent lobsters, high tech companies, brilliant university students, and world class medical care.

Tourism, finance, and education are among our specialties.

We import oil from OPEC, lend money in Latin America, and sell razor blades worldwide.

Our markets obey rules of the Boston City Council, the Commonwealth of Massachusetts, and the United States Congress.

Old and new merge in our landmarks—the John Hancock Tower, Fanueil Hall and Quincy Market, and the World Trade Center.

We were first with the Boston Latin School, the Boston Public Library, and the Boston Marathon.

Like other American cities we struggle to improve our schools and care for our homeless.

Welcome to Boston, USA.

GLOSSARY

Absolute Advantage—The ability of an individual, a business, or a nation to produce more of a product than another individual, business, or nation, using the same amount of resources.

Birth Rate—The total number of live births in a year for every 1000 people in a population. Sometimes called crude birth rate.

Capital Resources—Human-made goods such as tools, machines, or factories that are used to produce other goods and services.

Cartogram—A map that uses population, gross domestic product, or some other property to determine the size of an area. A typical map that shows country or state boundaries is a cartogram based on area in square miles.

Census—An official count of the population of the United States that is taken every ten years.

Change—Physical and human processes that operate to modify the earth's surface. Knowledge, ideologies, values, resources, and technology change and affect people's decisions about how to use land and how to organize society.

Choropleth Map—A map that displays data by political boundary. It shows differences between areas by using colors or shading to represent distinct categories of qualities (such as vegetation type) or quantities (such as Gross Domestic Product).

Cohort—Term used by demographers to designate people in the same age group.

Comparative Advantage—The ability of an individual, a business, or a nation to produce a product at a lower opportunity cost than another individual, business, or nation.

Consumer Goods—Goods and services that satisfy human wants directly.

Consumer Spending—The buying of goods and services by individuals and households to be used to satisfy wants.

Death Rate—The total number of deaths in a year for every 1000 people in a population. Sometimes called crude death rate.

Demand—The amounts of a good or service that buyers will be willing and able to buy at various prices during a given period of time.

Demography—The science dealing with statistics of human population, including size, distribution, diseases, births, and deaths.

Double Counting—The counting of intermediate goods (goods that are purchased for resale or further processing or manufacturing during the year) and the goods made from intermediate goods. Economists avoid double counting when measuring Gross Domestic Product by counting only final goods.

Earnings and Cost Approach—Measuring Gross Domestic Product by adding up the payments received by all those who contributed to production.

Ecological Perspective—A frame of reference for asking and answering questions, identifying and solving problems, and evaluating the consequences of alternative actions. The ecological perspective focuses on connections and relationships among life forms, ecosystems, and human societies.

Economic Institutions—The business organizations, labor unions, government agencies, laws and customs of a society that deal with scarcity and the way in which goods and services are produced, distributed, and consumed. Banks, minimum wage laws, and tipping are economic institutions in the United States.

Embargo—A ban on trade with other countries.

Emigration—Leaving one's own country or region to settle in another.

Environment—Everything in and on the earth's surface and its atmosphere within which organisms, communities, or objects exist.

Exchange Rate—The price of a nation's currency in terms of the currency of another nation.

Exports—Goods and services sold to foreign people, businesses, or governments.

Final Goods—Products that are made for consumption rather than as intermediate products used in the process of production.

Flow of Product Approach—Determining the Gross Domestic Product by adding the value of final goods and services received. Gross Domestic Product is equal to the sum of Consumption, Investment, Government, and Net Exports, using this approach.

Government Regulation—Government intervention in the economy to promote specific or general goals such as trying to correct for externalities, maintain competition, or redistribute income.

Gross Domestic Product (GDP)—The total market value of all final goods and services produced in an economy in a given year.

Gross Domestic Product Per Capita—A nation's Gross Domestic Product divided by the nation's population.

Gross State Product—The total market value of all final goods and services produced in a state's economy in a given year.

Gross State Product Per Capita—A state's Gross State Product divided by the state's population.

Hazardous Waste—Discarded materials of households and businesses that create potential health problems to vegetation, fish, animals, and humans.

Human Capital—The skills and knowledge embodied in the labor force.

Human-Environment Interaction—How humans interact with physical environments to form places. Humans use places for different activities that alter the physical features of these places.

Human Resources—The quantity and quality of human efforts directed toward producing goods and services.

Immigration—Coming to live in a foreign country.

Imports—Goods and services bought from sellers in another country.

Infant Industry—A new industry in a country that is not yet large enough to compete with established industries in other countries.

Infant Mortality—Deaths among infants under one year of age. An infant mortality rate is a measure of the number of deaths among infants under one year of age for every 1,000 live births.

International Trade—The exchange of goods and services between people and institutions in different countries.

Investment—Creation of new capital resources, sacrificing current consumption to increase expected production in the future.

Investment Spending—Spending on capital goods.

Invisible Exports—Services such as shipping, travel and tourism, insurance, and banking that are provided to people from other countries.

Licensing Requirements—Required of importers of foreign goods, so that imports can be restricted by limiting the number of licenses issued.

Life Expectancy—The average number of remaining years a person can expect to live. Life expectancy at birth is the most common use of this measure.

Location—The position of a point on the earth's surface expressed by means of a grid or in relation to the positions of other places.

Market Mechanism—The interaction of supply and demand in a free market economy, determining price and the allocation of resources.

Measure of Value—Using money to express the market value of different goods and services.

Median Age—A measure dividing an age distribution into two equal parts, one half of the cases falling below the median value and one half above the value.

Money—Something generally acceptable in payment for goods and services and in settling debts.

Movement—A concept used to analyze patterns of spatial organization. Both physical and human elements move.

National Capital—The city where the government of a country is officially located.

Natural Resources—The physical gifts of nature that are available without human intervention. The original fertility of land, mineral deposits, climate, water, and vegetation are natural resources. The value of most natural resources is usually realized when human labor and capital are used to process them.

Negative Relationship—When individuals, groups, or countries with high values for one variable have low values for the other variable.

Nonrenewable Resources—A finite resource that cannot be replaced once it is used up.

Opportunity Cost—The highest valued alternative that must be forgone because another option is chosen.

Place—A location having distinctive characteristics that give it meaning and character and distinguish it from other locations.

Population—The number of people living in any defined area.

Population Density—The number of individuals occupying an area divided by the area they occupy (10,000 people divided by 100 square miles would result in a population density of 100 people per square mile).

Population Growth—The percentage increase in population for a year or the average percentage increase over a period of years is an area's population growth rate. Populations grow when the number of births is greater than the number of deaths, or the number of immigrants is greater than the number of emigrants. If these two sources of population growth move in opposite directions, the larger effect determines the outcome.

Population Pyramid—A bar graph showing the distribution by gender and age of an area's population.

Positive Relationship—When individuals, groups, or countries with high values for one variable have high values for the other variable. Low values for both variables is a positive relationship, also.

Price—The amount of money that people pay when they buy a good or service.

Productive Resources—All natural resources, human resources, and human-made resources (capital) used in the production of goods and services.

Property Rights—The legal limits governing people's use and control of economic resources.

Quotas—Limits on the amounts of specific products that may be imported.

Range—The maximum distance and time people are willing to travel to purchase a good or service. (In statistics, the difference between the highest and the lowest values in a frequency distribution.)

Real Gross Domestic Product—Gross Domestic Product adjusted for price level changes.

Region—An area with one or more common characteristics or features that distinguish it from surrounding areas.

Renewable Resources—Resources that can be regenerated if used carefully.

Role of Government—Activities of the United States government to provide some goods and services; define and enforce property rights; provide standard units of weights, measures, and money; regulate economic activity to correct externalities and maintain competition; redistribute income; and promote full employment, stable prices, and economic growth.

Spatial Perspective—A frame of reference for asking and answering questions, identifying and solving problems, and evaluating the consequences of alternative actions.

Specialization—People, businesses, or nations producing those goods and services in which they have a comparative advantage.

Standards (health and safety)—Laws or regulations for imported goods, frequently much stricter than those applied to domestically produced goods.

Strategic Industry—An industry important for reasons of national security. It is frequently argued that these industries must be protected from foreign competition to ensure the availability of strategic materials in time of war.

Subsidies—Payments made to domestic producers to enable them to compete with foreign producers.

Supply—The amounts of a good or service that sellers will be willing and able to sell at various prices during a given period of time.

Tariffs—Taxes on imported goods that are imposed to raise revenue for the domestic government, or to protect domestic producers from foreign producers, or to provide some revenue and some protection.

Technology—Application of knowledge to meet the wants of people.

Terms of Trade—Quantity of goods and services that must be given up for one unit of goods and services received by each party to a transaction. The terms are equal to the ratio at which the goods and services are exchanged.

Third Party Costs—Costs of market transactions not fully paid by the direct producers and consumers of the goods and services. Air and water pollution are examples of third party costs.

Threshold—The minimum population needed for a business to succeed in a location.

Time-distance—The amount of time it takes to travel between two places.

Trade—The exchange of goods and services between people and institutions.

Transaction Costs—Those costs other than price associated with the purchase of a good or service. Legal restrictions on trading, costs of gathering or disseminating information on products, and transportation costs paid by the consumer are examples of transaction costs.

Value of Time—The opportunity cost of using time. Both consumption and production activities take time. When an hour is used for leisure or consumption activities, an opportunity cost of foregone income from working may be incurred.

Visible Exports—Exported merchandise or physical goods that can be counted.

SELECTED BIBLIOGRAPHY

Economic Report of the President, 1994. Washington, DC: Superintendent of Documents, 1994.

Encyclopedia Britannica Educational Corporation. *Britannica Global Geography System: Geographic Inquiry into Global Issues* (twenty print modules and multimedia). Chicago: Encyclopedia Britannica Educational Corporation, 1995.

Geography For Life: National Geography Standards, 1994. Washington, DC: National Geographic Research and Exploration, 1994.

Massachusetts Geographic Alliance. *Global Geography: Activities for Teaching the Five Themes of Geography.* Boulder, CO: Social Science Education Consortium, 1990.

National Council for the Social Studies. *Expectations of Excellence: Curriculum Standards for Social Studies.* Washington, DC: National Council for the Social Studies, 1994.

Natoli, Salvatore J., ed. *Strengthening Geography in the Social Studies.* Washington, DC: National Council for the Social Studies, 1988.

Pocket USA. London: The Economist Books, 1993.

Pocket World in Figures. London: The Economist Books, 1992.

Saunders, Phillip and June Gilliard, eds. *A Framework for Teaching Basic Economic Concepts with Scope and Sequence Guidelines, K–12.* New York: National Council on Economic Education, 1995.

Stoltman, Joseph P. *Geography Education for Citizenship.* Bloomington, IN: Social Studies Development Center, 1990.

United States Bureau of the Census. *1990 Census of Population, General Population Characteristics, Massachusetts.* Washington, DC: Superintendent of Documents, 1992. (There is a volume for each of the United States.)

United States Bureau of the Census. *1990 Census of Population, General Population Characteristics, United States.* Washington, DC: Superintendent of Documents, 1992.

United States Bureau of the Census. *Statistical Abstract of the United States, 1993* (113th edition). Washington, DC: Superintendent of Documents, 1993.

World Eagle: The Monthly Social Studies Resource. Littleton, MA: Independent Broadcasting Associates, Inc., 1995.